Copyright © 2015 Social Sales Link, LLC – All rights reserved.

LinkedIn & Social Selling For Business Development

Your On-Demand Webinar

Enjoy the LinkedIn & Social Selling Webinar!

LinkedInWebinar.info

Use password in back of book.

Brynne's Story

I began my sales career in the early '90s – no cell phones, no computers and lots of cold calling. However, I came to learn that my "real business" always came from client and networking referrals.

I recall sitting across from my client, staring at his overflowing Rolodex, thinking "If I could just get my hands on that for 20 minutes, I would be able to identify who he knows that he could introduce me to, and my business would boom!"

Fast forward two decades and my dream was answered – LinkedIn. An on-line Rolodex of all of my connections with the ability to filter and search my target market, and get the "warm" introductions to professionals that I would never have gotten through traditional cold calling.

Here is just one of my favorite stories: Robert Petcove, now Area Vice President at Arthur J. Gallagher and Co., hired us to teach his team how to leverage LinkedIn to grow their business. After our class he said, "Brynne, we learned a lot today and I want to put it to practice with you. Let's identify 30 people from each other's connections, review them with each other and make introductions."

So that is what we did. We each picked 30 names, whittled it down to 5 each, exchanged our introduction paragraphs and the fun began. I introduced Rob to some CFOs and he introduced me to some VP of Sales. One of the introductions Rob made for me was to Rob Curley at TD Bank. Rob Curley wasn't looking for training, but because his buddy Rob Petcove said we should meet, he gave me 30 minutes. It was clear that I was there only because of our mutual connection. In fact, I am 100% sure that if I had cold called Rob Curley I would never have gotten a meeting.

By the end of the 30 minutes, TD Bank was scheduling LinkedIn Training. In the class, when we were reviewing the templates from our first book, Rob Curley began to laugh, "The introduction paragraph that Rob Petcove made to us is verbatim. I thought it was personalized! Too funny." I looked at Rob Curley and said, "I am here, right? It works!"

In 2008, I started teaching LinkedIn and social media to folks in transition, business owners and sales professionals. It really began as a prospecting and branding class and six years later it has morphed into an entire new way of selling. But it isn't limited to LinkedIn. LinkedIn is by far the foundational tool, but it takes a village to raise a sales team. So was born Social Sales Link, the missing link between traditional sales training and social media.

Social Selling is a quintessential part of identifying, researching, meeting, relating and growing a client relationship. It certainly begins with prospecting, marketing and lead generation, but it is ever evolving throughout the entire sales cycle.

In this book we will cover what a business-to-business marketing and sales departments need to be doing to grow their business with today's buyers. Get ready to fill the sales funnel with better leads through introductions and thought leadership; schedule more qualified appointments; prepare for sales calls using social media productively; leverage knowledge and research to best position your solution; and close more business. Welcome to social selling.

Foreword

LinkedIn's Global Senior Social Marketing Manager, Koka Sexton

The evolution of social selling.

The business of selling has always been social. Though the end results of generating new revenue are still the same, the tactics like anything in life must change to meet the current landscape.

A brief history of sales.

The art of bartering is sales in its earliest form; for the most part it was transactions between people from different villages, tribes or communities. Each with their own resources they would use to exchange for other resources. It was a trying process that would sometimes require long journeys across land and sea.

This person-to-person contact built strong relationships, developed confidence on the side of the buyer and seller and with something as symbolic as a handshake, sales people would put their reputation on the line for their product or service.

The modern telemarketing call center was created and entire phone banks were built to leverage the ability to connect with customers at a scale unheard of just a short time earlier.

The evolution of modern sales.

As the 21st century rolled in, email was becoming more prevalent. I remember one of my first jobs where email was just starting to be used. It was actually a heavily debated topic with the leadership team if sales people would have access to email or if it should be reserved for only the executives.

Can you imagine not having email?

Email became the new tool for sales people to communicate with prospects without having to go door to door or hoping to reach them on the phone. Unfortunately this new tool was relied upon too heavily and the ultimate result of trying to play the numbers game was labeled SPAM.

Not so long ago I was a sales rep carrying a quota in a highly competitive market. It was clear to me then that the sales tactics being passed down from my predecessors was not working. Dialing for dollars and pitching anyone that would answer the phone was a losing battle. I had to make an important decision; do I keep down the losing path or do I get off the beaten trail and do something radically different and surely disruptive?

Inevitability of social selling

This brings us to our newest sales tool, social media. Not just a tool for marketing, social media becomes a precision instrument for social selling. The art of listening and engagement at a global scale can be very profitable if done right.

The social buying process has turned sales sideways and given more control over to the buyer. Buyers no longer have to get information from sales people, they can self educate, research best of breed technologies and ask their trusted connections for recommendations.

Now instead of having lengthy discovery calls, sales professionals are expected to have social insights on their prospects and an understanding of what's going on in the industry.

These new trends have led to the executives even following other executives' social profiles in an attempt to stay connected, informed, and available for collaboration whenever it's feasible.

The age of social selling is upon us. High performing companies like IBM, ADT and Oracle among others are already reaping the financial and brand benefits of empowering their sales teams with training in social selling and access to the best tools available.

The world's largest professional network, LinkedIn, now has 259 million members and growing at the rate of nearly two new members a second.

Do you think B2B buyers are going to stop getting connected with other professionals in their industry?

There are now 5.7 billion people searches each year on LinkedIn and growing rapidly. Is that number going to reverse course?

Do we think plummeting cold call rates are going to suddenly stabilize and then reverse course and get better? Today cold call rates are 3% effective and dropping. Tomorrow do we believe they'll get better and get to 5% and then to 10% success and beyond?

Are plunging email response rates going to improve? Do we really think that as the volume of email increases exponentially, we're going to reverse course and soon our reps will enjoy far higher email response rates? And by the way, voice mail response rates will start soaring back up too?

In such a world, isn't it inevitable that your sales reps will be at a severe disadvantage without LinkedIn, how could they do their jobs without it?

This book from Brynne Tillman encapsulates the social selling ethos. Page after page of tips and best practices for sales professionals. I see this as a workbook and the most up to date reference material for sales people learning to leverage LinkedIn. Keep this book on your desk, the information within will provide value for a long time.

Why LinkedIn?

As sales trainers and social marketers we are frequently asked questions about LinkedIn. The most common question we get is "So I signed up on LinkedIn, but I don't know what I'm supposed to do with it. Is it really worth my time? Here are some statistics that we found astounding.

- LinkedIn reported that as of October 2013, it had more than 259 million members (63% of the members are from outside of the US and represent 19 languages) and that there are 2.6 million companies represented.

- There are approximatly 154 million monthly visitors, from 200 countries, speaking 20 different languages.

- 38% are mobile visitors, 40% of users check LinkedIn daily, and there are more than three million LinkedIn business pages.

- There are 2.1 million groups with 8,000 new groups created weekly, the average user spends seventeen minutes on LinkedIn.

- The rate of web traffic referrals is 34.51% - that means that over 1/3 of traffic to B2B websites initiate through LinkedIn!

- The average age of the LinkedIn user is 37-years old, with $61k in income.

- Every Fortune 5000 company is listed/represented on LinkedIn.

With statistics like these, it's clear this is where all the right people are hanging out.

LinkedIn gives us the opportunity to search and filter these members and identify who we know that knows who we want to know, and get warm introductions.

We have learned that when you know how to use LinkedIn well, not only does it position your business to be a competitive force, but it positions the individual as the subject matter expert, thought leader and a center of influence.

LinkedIn is not the new way of networking, it is an essential tool that enhances the traditional way of networking to be more productive, purposeful and time saving. Yes, time saving. Often we hear, "How do you have time to do all this LinkedIn stuff?" Our answer is: if you do what you learn, you won't have time not to do it. The return on invested time is unprecedented.

If you hunt for new business or are responsible for client acquisition, this book could quite possibly change the way you grow your business forever.

Why Social Selling?

First, what is social selling? We went to Wikipedia today to get a definition to share with you, and guess what? It isn't even there yet. So maybe in our free time we will add it...unless you beat us to it. So, we are on the cutting edge – right here, right now. We are defining Social Selling as social media imbedded into the fabric of a companie's sales process. It is bridging the gap between the marketing department and the sales department, in fact, when done well; the two will be friends again. Why?

- Social Selling is a lead generation machine. It attracts and engages our prospective clients through thought leadership and content that provokes critical thinking. It educates the consumer before we ever even know they exist. When our prospects are searching for information on what we do and what we sell, they find us because we are social selling.

- It is a key piece of the information gathering and pre-call planning. We can learn incredible insights into our prospects and identify their core mission and values from what we find on twitter, LinkedIn, Google, web pages, press releases and so much more. We can gain knowledge on what is important to their organization right now, what initiatives they are running and what success they are proud of. Bridging what we learn into our conversations and selling process proves that we are on the pulse of what matters to them which ultimately strengthens our relationships.

- With the power of LinkedIn we can leverage our connections. Through advanced searches we can identify connections that we have in common and make some phone calls. We can learn about them personally and leverage those relationships to create immediate rapport. In addition, we can search prior employees of the company and even the specific department you are selling into, learn about their experiences, and gain inside knowledge of the selling process and how they made buying decisions in the past. This is inside information that you could never get anywhere else.

- We can gain incredible information about industry trends. Through just a little bit of research, it is simple to understand what is going on in our prospect's world. We can read influential blogs that matter to our prospects, find out how the company's stock price is doing and what the trend has been. Research their competitor's. Identify if there have been mergers or acquisitions for them or in the industry as a whole. You can find an annual report or press-release. You can even do a little search on the job boards to see if the company and/or industry is hiring.

- Social Selling is referral selling. LinkedIn is an online Rolodex of all of our connection's connections – and we can search and filter to identify whom they know that we want to know. Then we need to ask for the referral. When our client says, "I love working with you." You say, "I am so glad, happy clients are a great thing. Mr. Client, I was wondering if you knew of anyone else that could benefit from my services the same way you do?" (AND THEN YOU GET THE BLANK STARE). They say, "I can't think of anyone right now, but if someone should ask, I would be happy to make an introduction. Here's the game changer: Instead of saying, "okay," you say, "I hope you don't mind, but I noticed you were connected to a few people on LinkedIn that would be a good introduction, can I run the names by you?" -Home Run! Touch Down! Goal!

Our business-to-business social selling philosophies are grounded in LinkedIn. Knowing how to use and leverage LinkedIn is the core to social selling, so that is where we will begin.

How To Use This Book

This book is designed to be used as a guide so that you can leverage LinkedIn from a business development perspective, the same way our students and clients have done with great success. We have filled the pages with strategies, tactics, techniques and customized templates, as well as LinkedIn's step-by-step instructions on navigation. We highly recommend that you work with this book alongside your live profile on LinkedIn.

We welcome you to start from the beginning and work your way through the step-by-step path leading to success. Or, you are welcome to hop around and learn sections that are pertinent to your personal goals.

Throughout your journey, you will find icons that can help you identify specific areas within the book:

Email Template   **Conversation**   **To Do**   **Stories**   **Ideas**

The best way to achieve success with this book is to keep it next to your computer and implement the steps as you read. We recommend that you take notes, earmark the pages and write in the margins. When you identify a tactic that you would like to implement in your business development efforts, write it on the "You Get Out of It What You Put Into It" page. The goal is that this activity becomes part of your daily activity and rapidly fills your pipeline quickly with qualified prospects on a consistent basis.

Table of Contents

Your Profile	11
Company Page	33
LinkedIn Publishing	41
Your Homepage	49
Your Connections	55
Your Groups	71
Your Network	81
Research and Insights	99
Social Selling	105
Your Plan	113
Extra Credit	127
Webinar Password	141

The Network

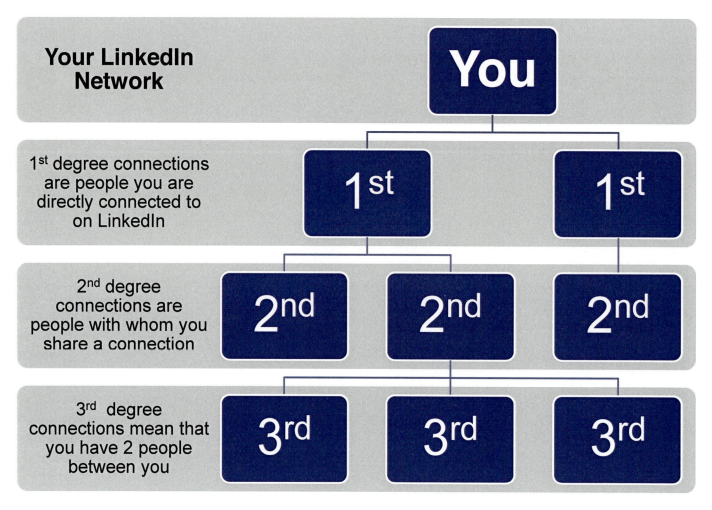

1st connections are people that you are connected to directly. One of you invited the other to join your respective LinkedIn network and the other accepted. You have access to their email and contact information and the ability to message them directly within LinkedIn.

2nd connections are often limited in what you can see on their profile depending on the individual settings. With the free account, the only way you can "direct message" them is if you share a group. This, however, is where we see the magic of LinkedIn. These professionals share a connection with us. They are a friend of a friend and we have the ability to leverage those relationships to get warm introductions to the individuals we want to meet.

3rd connections are cold, and the only way to send them a message from a free account is if you share a group. We don't spend much time on the 3rd degree connections as the true magic within LinkedIn lives within 2nd degree connections.

You Get Out What You Put Into It

Our commitment to give you the tools you need to leverage LinkedIn and social selling for business development starts here. We will offer you sales tools, scripts, strategies and tactics to make prospecting fun and productive. As you go through this book, your responsibility is to come up with a few strategies to implement that will make an impact on your sales activity.

As you come across specific tactics that you know will benefit the growth of your business, write them down on the list below. At the end of this book we are going to work on activity and results goal planning. So for now, just enter the goal. Later we will handle the Priority, Smart and Goal Type sections.

Social Selling To Do List	PRIORITY A B C	SMART Y/N	GOAL A/R
1.			
2.			
3.			
4.			
5.			
6.			
7.			
8.			
9.			
10.			

Just to cure curiosity, SMART is an acronym for Specific, Measurable, Aligned with company goals, Realistic and Time bound and Goal Type: A= Activity goals R= Results goals. Results goals are what you plan to happen. Activity goals are what you do to make it happen. (You get priority right?)

Your Profile

Creating a Client Centric Profile

Have you ever been to a live networking meeting? Did you know that when someone walks through the door, you make a decision on whether or not you want to meet that person within 7 seconds? Guess what? On LinkedIn you have 3 seconds to make a strong enough impression for your viewer to continue to read on and ultimately engage. Keep in mind that this is the ultimate purpose of your LinkedIn profile: to get a next step on the calendar (often a phone call or meeting). Our LinkedIn strategy for B2B sales professionals is founded in two distinct ways:

First, the activity centered on the power of your personal network and getting warm introductions to the people you want to meet. Whether we are working with networking partners or clients, LinkedIn, used correctly, will make asking and getting referrals into our targeted prospects easier. Our clients tell us that when using our LinkedIn strategy they are getting the competitive advantage they need. Not only are they securing more qualified appointments but also their sales cycle is reduced significantly and they are closing more business. In fact, often they are not even up against other competitors as they have already been vetted out by your common connection, the referral source. The prospect feels that because you came to them so highly recommended, the choice to hire you is solely based on whether or not they need your products and services, not whether you are the right one to do it.

Second, is the marketing aspect. Getting on the radar of targeted prospects through thought leadership is the key to attracting your prospects to your profile. The foundation of this entails branding you and your company as the subject matter experts. This marketing tactic is centered around educational content. This strategy takes a little more time then the former tactic of warm market introductions, and it has a significant impact on getting your message out virally to create inbound leads.

Because this is done through LinkedIn, the very first thing that is going to happen is that your profile is going to be getting a significant amount of traffic. This often is your first impression, and so it better be well-thought out. This is your opportunity to get your message across and to communicate the right story so that at a glance, your prospect is looking to learn more.

Whether or not you decide to actively use LinkedIn, your profile is out there and is still representing you, your company and your brand. Did you ever Google yourself? If you don't have a felony, the first thing that comes up is your LinkedIn profile. So, at a minimum your profile needs to tell your story in a way that attracts your prospects to you. "What is in it for them?" and "Why should they work with you?" are the foundation of the profile message. It is critical that in addition to the message, your profile needs to be told in an authentic voice and represent you as a professional and as an individual. When a prospect meets you, his or her experience needs to be aligned with the impression they derived from LinkedIn.

Obviously having the right content is important, but equally important is that you use the key words and phrases so that you can be found. LinkedIn is indexed heavily by Google, so let's play by the search engine rules – we want to be found…right?

Search Engine Optimization

Search engine optimization is the process of affecting the visibility of a website or a web page in a search engine's "natural" or un-paid ("Organic") search results. In general, the earlier (or higher ranked on the search results page) and more frequently a site appears in the search results list, the more visitors it will receive from the search engine's users. SEO may target different kinds of searches, including image search, local search, video search, academic search, news search and industry-specific vertical search engines. – Wikipedia

We need to make a list of key words and phrases that we believe our prospects are using to find our products and/or services. Then we want to check to see if they really are the words and phrases they use in their searches. There are many sites that can help you to identify and determine some strategic words that you will want to include throughout your profile so you can be found, here are a few to check out:

wordstream.com/keywords – there is a free version available but it gives you limited information. They claim to have a trillion-keyword database and you can try 30 keywords for free. There are checkboxes that allow you to filter and more options for finding negative keywords and grouping your keywords. The full paid version has tens of thousands of results for many keywords, the top 100 of which are available for free.

semrush.com is the king of keyword search – however only the first 10 are free, so use them wisely. SEMrush also shares 10 organic competitors for those keywords. Visit those competitors' profiles and get the 10 organic keywords they are ranking for. You gain great insight into the words and phrases that you should be using.

adwords.google.com - Click on tools and analytics. Type in your keyword and you get to see how many times those terms were searched.

http://www.keywordeye.com - This is our favorite; it gives you word clouds and graphs and all kinds of fun tools to help you assess your keywords. They have a basic free and a pro version. No need to pay initially, the basic will give you 10 searches, so use them wisely. You will have to sign up and confirm your email, and then you are all set.

http://www.keywordspy.com/ - LOVE this! The magic here is in discovering your competitors and their keywords, daily database updates, looking into good adwords and sharing with you who is buying those keywords, and ultimately profiting from the success of your competitors. Sign up for the free trial.

If you have had a website developer, there is a good chance they can provide this information for you.

How They Search for You

Be sure to include keywords at least in 5 key areas of the profile:

1. Your headline
2. Your job titles and descriptions (past and present)
3. Your summary
4. Your projects and publications and keyword terms in your media attachments
5. Skills and Endorsements

Keywords and Phrases
1.
2.
3.
4.
5.
6.
7.
8.
9.
10.

Google some of the words, don't just rely on the SEO keyword sites. If you are looking for a true search without your cookies or history distorting the findings, simply go incognito on Chrome. Click on the three horizontal bars at the top right and then open an incognito tab and your searches will be organic.

LinkedIn & Social Selling For Business Development

What is your value proposition? What do you bring to the table?
Why do your clients need you, want you, use you?

Value Proposition

1.
2.
3.
4.
5.

What are 3 tips that you can offer your prospects that make them go wow?
Things that they can do without you, not tips that sell you.

Three Tips

1.

2.

3.

Headshot

Let's talk about the first thing people see when they get to your profile, that 3 second glance. It is your picture and your headline. A professional picture is critical for engagement, people connect with people, with smiles, with a sparkle in your eyes, and a professional picture best captures that. We often say only use a picture that you would put on your website. We don't care how much you love your Hawaiian shirt, your dog or that wedding photo cut out with your spouse's hand on your shoulder, those belong on Facebook!

If you really want your picture to pop, put a border around it. You can pop the photo into PowerPoint, double click on the photo, click border, color and line weight then right click save as picture. Upload it and you are done. It will start to brand you a little bit. So whether you match the color of your logo, or just pick your favorite color, it will stand out in many areas on LinkedIn.

Headline

Headline is where we begin to add value. Many people have their job title and their company in their headline. Even if it did say who you are, if you reach out to someone to get an introduction and they check out your profile and they see you're in sales, are they taking your call? Probably not because they know you want to sell them. So what do they care about?

In one class, a gentleman had, Sales Manager and the name of his company in his headline. When asked how he helps his clients, he said, "We let people utilize technology to get more done in less time as far as manufacturing and distribution companies. We leverage technology to get more accomplished in the world we currently live in."

"So, how about this in your headline?" "Helping manufacturing and distribution companies leverage technology to be more effective." That is your value proposition. So if you are a manufacturing person and you get an introduction, is that way more interesting to you? If you are in manufacturing you probably would like to learn how to be more productive, and you know that might be worth a conversation. Another option is "Learn 3 ways manufacturing and distribution companies leverage technology to be more effective by reading my summary." This piques curiosity, creates immediate engagement and gets them to your summary section to read the tips. Be sure to make them good ones! This is your three seconds, so make the most of it.

You've got 120 characters for your headline, it is valuable real estate, make every character count.

You may want to consider adding a few symbols to spice it up! Throughout my LinkedIn training career I have worked on thousands of profile makeovers. Adding symbols was always a point of debate. Was it too goofy, too high school, too unprofessional, or did it catch the eye, bring people in, and get people interested? Well, it is still the topic of discussion, but I do believe if used well and sparingly, symbols have their place on the LinkedIn profile. For a list of symbols that are easy to copy and paste visit: bit.ly/LinkedInSymbols (case sensitive).

LinkedIn & Social Selling For Business Development

Background Banner

Leveraging this great branding opportunity is key to the first impression your profile visitors have, so make the most of it. Be sure to include your phone number, website or maybe even your email in your banner, as the goal of your profile is to get engagement, so this helps make it easy to get in contact with you.

Background images must be:
- File type JPG, GIF or PNG
- No larger than 4MB.
- Pixel Dimensions between 1000 X 425 and 4000 X 4000 ideally 1400 x 425 pixels

BONUS: A professional graphic is important, but if you don't have a designer visit Fiverr.com or Canva.com – you will be amazed at what you get for under $10.

Summary

Once we are branding, marketing, networking and asking for referrals on LinkedIn, the first thing that's going to happen is we're going to get a lot more traffic to our profile. So let's focus here. But first, what is the purpose of our profile?

To engage your reader, to get people to raise their hand and talk to you. We need to make sure that our profile is telling the right story, the story that our prospects want to hear, not what we want to tell them. What excites them? What engages them? What value do you bring to the conversation? Why should they want to raise their hand? And the best place to do this is in your summary.

In the Social Selling world it is about education and thought leadership, so our LinkedIn profile is no different. If we are in a business development role, we need to start showing our value immediately, and that starts in our profile. There are two common profiles that just don't have the impact we're looking for. First is the resume profile, now if you are looking for a job, go for it. But if you are looking to engage prospects, do you really think your detailed CV will get them all pumped up about talking with you? Second is the market profile, and it is all about their products and services, their message about how they can help hundreds of people just like me, and how I should call them so they can sell me stuff. Not so excited about this one either. So, what kind of profile works? A Social Selling profile, a profile filled with stuff for them, like tips, strategies, education and ideas that clearly add value from the very first engagement. If they have a wow moment on your profile, they will raise their hand to talk with you.

If you are not looking for a job, this does not need to be your resume. This is your landing page just like a website. Even if someone else employs you, but you're responsible for business development, treat your position as if you were an entrepreneur. You're responsible for growing your own business, so this page allows you to get the message out the way you would like to be represented. Often people push back and say "oh but this is my personal page." Your Facebook page is your personal page. This is your professional page so if you are in sales, then this is the place to market yourself. Unless you are actively looking for a new position, use LinkedIn to grow your business, make more money and be represented as a professional.

Your summary is your value proposition drilled down. It's our goal that when your viewers read it, they want more, they raise their hand and say, "talk to me". We want engagement. In both of our summaries, we have decided to add value through LinkedIn tips. That is actually the first thing each of our profile visitors will read, so we need to be sure that these tips will bring great value and brand us as industry leaders. If we begin with a summary that explains who we are and what we do, then it is about what we want to tell them which is rarely what they want to hear. If we lead with what is important to them, we become important to them. Marketing 101 – let's bring it to LinkedIn.

Also, make sure you add your website, phone number and email address. Only your 1st degree connections can see all your information in your contact box, and we want to be sure that your 2nds and 3rds can reach you easily.

Media

LinkedIn supports many types of media to be displayed on your profile. You can upload a file or link a URL to your profile. This can include PowerPoint presentations, videos, .PDF files and many more. Links can come from your website, YouTube or any other hosting source. If you have media that need a URL, you can utilize SlideShare.com. It is free to set up an account and with a simple upload, your collateral has its own URL.

Check out SoundCloud.com. You can record any audio for free and then upload a message to your LinkedIn page.

Other great resources are Wordpress.com, Box.net, SlideShare and Dropbox.com. You can upload your own media and it is assigned its own URL.

 To add any media, click on this icon in sections including:

1. Summary
2. Experience (available for every position listed)
3. Education

Video

Having video on LinkedIn is an important asset when connecting with your profile viewers. Whether used as a reminder to someone after they have met you or viewed as a first impression, a video is your opportunity to make a lasting impression.

If you talk with any website developer, they will tell you video is very important. It is even more so in your LinkedIn profile. In addition to it helping you grow your brand, it is a very powerful SEO feature.

Although it is easy to record a video from a camera or smartphone, we recommend getting your video professionally done. You want your branding to represent you completely. It is also important to have a script and to be well prepared. There is one goal of this video…it is to get a prospect to want to talk with you. Here are the critical elements that make a successful LinkedIn video:

1. Be sure it is clear that you are a thought leader and a subject matter expert.
2. Get your story out.
3. Show passion for what you do.
4. Offer industry insights.
5. Get them thinking.
6. Leave them with an "aha" moment.

Although we highly recommend professional video, you can convert a PowerPoint or Prezi Presentation into a video with a voice over recording. Whether you create it inside PowerPoint or use a screen recording software like QuickTime, it is a very inexpensive way to get a message across.

Genre

There are five types of videos that create engagement on LinkedIn profiles.

1. **For the job seekers.** Create a three minute introduction. This is an opportunity for you to pre-interview with a recruiter or hiring manager. Be sure that this is done professionally and with a message about what you bring to the table for a client.

2. **A welcome video.** "Thank you for visiting my profile, here's who I am and how I add value." This video turns any profile visit into a warm one. It is also a great way for people to remember who you are. If we go to a networking event, and meet 11 people, no matter how sure we are that we will remember someone, by the next day all of the cards blend together. We will follow up and connect on LinkedIn, and if there is a video, we can recall our conversation from the night before immediately. As we go through this book, we are going to focus a lot on warm introductions from both clients and networking partners. What better way for them to explain what you do than to say, hey, go look at Brynne's LinkedIn profile and watch her video to learn a bit more about her. When it's time for the phone call, my prospect is already warmed up!

3. **Testimonial videos.** Have a professional video person at your next class, client appreciation event, holiday party or gathering and have them ask your clients one or two poignant questions that can become great sound bites for a video. Nothing sells you better than other people's praises.

4. **Project Demo.** This includes realtors and architects and designers. Show your product demonstrations or a virtual tour. If you are a trainer or speaker, you are the product, show it off here.

5. **Education**. We are firm believers that if you bring value to someone you begin to matter. The sales world has changed significantly over the past decade. It used to be that in order for a prospect to learn about your business you had to meet with them in person or at minimum have a phone conversation so they can learn about your products and services. Now they're checking out Google and they're checking out all the possible vendor choices (your competition) and they are reading content. This content is forming their options, their wants and needs and their perspective on your industry. You want your content to be some of what they're checking out. You want to be molding their purchasing decisions and swaying them to your techniques and methodologies. And the best way to do this is to bring them value. Don't sell here ever because it is an education piece, but absolutely have a call to action, a next step. We have a video called 5 LinkedIn Video Tips so You NEVER have to Cold Call Again that is chapterized. After the 1st tip we ask for an email address. It isn't required, but many people find that 1st tips so compelling that they are happy to share their information with me. You can invite them to connect with you on LinkedIn or even have a conversation, but either way this is a fabulous way to get qualified leads of people who are truly interested in your thought leadership. This, by the way, is quintessential social selling. It's just purely education.

Use a video lead capture program like Wistia. You can ask for opt-ins with an email address before, in the middle or at the end of a video. The statistics are astounding and can truly make an impact on your marketing and sales goals. Add a second click link inside the video and you really begin to see engagement.

Profile Sections

Honors and Awards- Add personal honors and awards. This is a wonderful way to post bragging rights and offer credibility to prospects and networking partners.

Organizations- Whether you are a member of a networking group, chamber of commerce or business association, listing it on your profile will help others understand more about you and your professional interests.

Volunteer & Causes- If you volunteer, it is so powerful to list this on your profile. It is a good representation of what is important to you and sends a message of community and self-less work ethic.

Courses- If the courses you have taken are relevant to your job, list them. The more experience in core areas, the better. You can choose classes from past and present education as well as companies that you may have taken class through or with.

Customize Your URL- This finishes off the look of your profile box. Simply choose your name and if it is available, it is yours. Your new URL for your profile is www.linkedin.com/in/YOURNAME - you can use it on your email signature, your business cards and your website.

When you are in your profile, you will find additional sections that you will add to your profile on the top right hand side of the page. When you click the plus sign next to the topic the section will automatically open and give you the opportunity to complete your information.

Drag and drop your up and down arrow to move your sections in the order in which you want your viewer to do them.

Develop Your Public Profile

Everyone has 2 profiles. The one that you and others see when they are logged into LinkedIn and the other is your public profile. This is what they see when they Google you and they are not logged into LinkedIn. Your public profile settings will allow you to control what people see, even outside of your network. On the right-hand side you can check and uncheck the sections that you would like your network to view. As you make those changes, you will immediately see them.

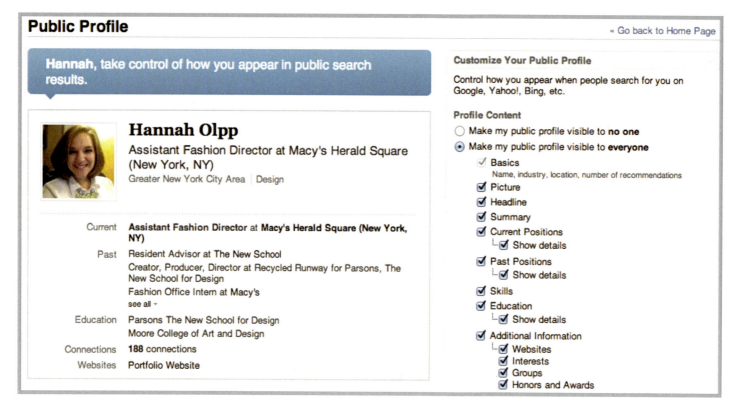

Log out of LinkedIn, then type in your public profile to see what others see when they view you.

LinkedIn & Social Selling For Business Development

Contact Information

Have you ever visited a website and tried to contact the company, but the site only showed a form without an email or phone number? It is so frustrating! It is critical that your visitors never feel this way. Make it easy for them to contact you. Your default email should be here already, but add your phone number, address and other relevant contact information as well.

You can connect to Twitter from here, which is a great tool for sharing your updates with the world. Plus, you can add up to 3 website links.

Do you have 3 websites? No worries if you answered no, because you can add 3 different pages on your website. Link your blogs, contact forms, event registration pages– anything that has a URL.

Here is how:

1. Go to the page you want to direct your prospects to on your website.
2. Highlight and copy the URL in the search bar.
3. Click Edit Contact Info on your profile.
4. Click pencil next to website
5. From drop down choose Other.
6. Type in the name of the page.
7. Paste URL and Save

If you would like to track the number of clicks here or anywhere you enter a URL try using a URL shortener like Bit.Ly or Owl.Ly. This is a great way to customize your link names, shorten them for messages and email campaigns as well as track how many people actually click through them. This is great marketing intelligence.

Location

We recommend that if you live in the suburbs or rural area, choose the larger city choice rather than the town that is connected to your zip code. This will help you show up in broader searches.

Industry

Your listed Industry is also important in searches, so listing the most suitable industry is critical to your SEO (Search Engine Optimized) profile. You are limited to a short list. Do your best to pick the most relevant. We do recommend that you choose the industry your company is in, not your title. For example, if you are in the marketing department of an IT Managed Services company, you might list Computer and Network Security (not Marketing and Advertising.)

Experience / Education

Add all of your educational experience that relates to your professional development. Even if you don't have degrees, you want to be sure your educational experience is on your profile. You don't need a full resume on your profile unless you are in job-search mode. Here, you can have a simplified version of your resume that just includes bullet points of your job responsibilities but, we recommend that you add your value proposition here as well as how you help your clients. List all your relevant positions based on your listed experiences and dates. LinkedIn will suggest people you may know that worked at your past companies during the same tenure. LinkedIn's profile adds more than just the name of the company in the Experience section. If there's a company page listed and you connect to it, LinkedIn will display the company logo on your Experience section. If you do not see a logo, edit your position, begin typing the company name and choose the correct link from the drop down.

Additional Information

The Contact info box isn't the only place to add your information. In fact there is one place that is open to everyone on LinkedIn to see additional information. This means that if someone finds your profile but is not in your network, they can get in touch with you – this is really important.

Interests are important to list because it helps others to get to know you personally. You can add personal detail such as birthday and marital status. It is certainly an individual choice, as it doesn't have an impact on business development activities.

Projects

LinkedIn Projects is a great way to showcase some of the work you and your company have done. You can name your project, add dates, additional team members and project description. A URL link to project information is available too. This is a fantastic area for marketing professionals to showcase their websites and collateral. This is also a great section for adding case studies.

Projects is a fantastic area for marketing professionals to showcase their websites and collateral. This is also a great section for adding case studies. Here is a simple case study layout that you are welcome to use as a guide:

Client:
Healthcare Insurance Company in the Greater Philadelphia Area

Driver:
Due to the shift in the healthcare environment and the change in broker compensation, it was critical for our client to sign on a few new clients to not just maintain their revenue but grow.

Challenge:
Client had difficulty identifying the influencers and decision makers in their target market (Fortune 1000 companies). Even when they did find the right people, getting past the gatekeeper was nearly impossible due to the endless call volume and the enormous competition in the industry.

Solution:
We identified all the possible titles of the influencers and decision makers in the human resource departments, created saved searches with the accurate criteria including company size, location, and common connections. Once we identified key prospects we created messaging templates and a social selling plan to engage and connect. We then converted new connections to initial phone calls with strategic follow-up.

Result:
Over a 6-month period, our clients had 27 new meaningful, scheduled conversations with decision makers that converted to 8 face-to-face appointments and 3 new clients.

With permission from your client, you can add them to the the project and then it will be linked to their profile as well.

By offering specific situations that showcase your expertise in solving problems that your prospects can relate to, you are establishing your capabilities in your space and positioning yourself to be the vendor of choice.

Skills & Endorsements

This is typically where we get eyes rolling in class. This is the "you've been endorsed for" section. So many people are getting endorsed for things they don't do by people they don't remember. Let us explain what is happening. The purpose of this section was initially created for recruiters. Prior to Skills & Endorsements, if a hiring manager or recruiter wanted to find someone with Microsoft Excel experience there wasn't an easy way to find them. So LinkedIn created the Skills section so the searches were much more robust. Then the recruiters asked how they would know if the candidates would be good at the skills they had listed, so LinkedIn responded with endorsements. Unfortunately, the way it was rolled out was in a way that people were endorsing people just because they were showing up in big blue boxes on their screen saying "Does Rich have all these skills?" endorse here. And many people do. We actually only endorse people that we're confident do a good job. We are spending our political capital and reputation and it is important to us that we stay authentic.

To add skills in your Skills & Endorsements section:

1. When in edit profile, scroll down to the Skills & Expertise section and click the edit icon in the top right.
2. Type the name of a skill and then choose it from the dropdown list that appears. If your skill doesn't appear, completely type in the skill name in the field.
3. Click Add.
4. Click Save.

Adding and Removing Skills.

You can add and remove skills from the Skills & Endorsements section. It is important to list relevant skills on your profile that will allow someone to understand your value and strengths. Also, because this section was developed for search capabilities, Google indexes this section so it is important for SEO purposes to optimize the keywords here.

You can add up to 50 skills to your profile. By default, skills with the most endorsements will be listed first. You can reorder your skills to be listed in the order you wish for them to be seen. When in edit profile, scroll down to the Skills & Endorsements section and click the edit icon in the top right. Then drag and drop the skills so that they appear in the order you prefer. Click Save. When you return to your profile, your skills will be listed in the new order you have created.

LinkedIn & Social Selling For Business Development

To remove skills in your Skills & Endorsements section:

1. When in edit profile, scroll down to the Skills & Endorsements section and click the edit icon in the top right.
2. Click the X next to any skill to remove it or drag and rearrange any skills without endorsements.
3. Click Save.

Manage your endorsements. You can control who shows up on your endorsements and who doesn't. If you are endorsed by someone and you would prefer that it not show, you can manage your endorsements.

You can choose to hide or unhide your skill endorsements.

1. When in edit profile, scroll down to the Skills & Endorsements section and click the edit icon in the top right.
2. Click the Manage Endorsements link. This is next to Add & Remove.
3. Click on a skill in the left column to reveal the connections who endorsed you for that skill. You may need to use the scroll bar on the left side of the box to view skills further down in the list.
4. Uncheck the box next to any people whose endorsements you want to hide. Or, check the box next to any you want to unhide.
5. Click Save.
6. Click Done editing in the top section of your profile.

If you are in an industry such as Financial Services and you are restricted from having endorsements show, you can hide all of your endorsements by default. This will keep all existing and new endorsements from ever displaying on your profile.

If someone endorses you for a skill, you are not obligated to endorse them back. In fact, unless you know that they are good at a skill then we recommend that you don't endorse. However, it is great to acknowledge them by sending a quick little note, and if it is a prospect, take advantage of this opportunity.

Hover over their picture next to the skill they endorsed you for click send message:

XXX, thank you very much for the endorsement, it means a lot to me. It has been some time since we have connected on LinkedIn and I thought it might make sense for us to set up a phone call. Please let me know if you have some time Thursday afternoon. If not, kindly send some alternatives. I am looking forward to catching up with you.

Brynne

Recommendations

There is no better way to get a prospect interested in you than for them to see how you have helped others. Your recommendations are more powerful than any other sales pitch you could make. Not only does your prospect get to see what your clients have said about you, but they can also click through to see their name, title and company information. Back in the day when we were about to sign a new client on to our business, we would be asked for references. This often took days, if not weeks, while your prospect and your client played phone tag with each other. Now, when a prospect asks us for a client reference, we can send them to our LinkedIn Recommendations, have them read through them, and choose which clients they would like to speak with. Since we have been doing this, we rarely have had a prospect come back to us with an introduction request. They have enough recommendations from a diverse group of professionals to be satisfied that we are successful in our field.

1. When in edit mode go to the bottom of your profile and click the pencil next to recommendations.
2. Click Ask to be recommended.
3. Select a position in the "Choose what you want to be recommended for" drop down menu.
4. Select a connection – gives you the option to ask for multiple recommendations at one time. We recommend you do one at a time and customize your message when making the request.
5. Click Send.

When requesting a recommendation, we suggest you have a conversation with the person first. The best recommendations come from clients and supervisors.

A perfect time to ask for a recommendation is when someone says something nice about you and your work – simply say:

"Thank you for the kind words, they mean a lot to me. Currently, I am building out my LinkedIn profile and a testimonial like that would be fantastic. Would you be open to writing what you just said in LinkedIn? If so, I could send you a link. If it is easier for you, I could try to summarize what you said and send that to you as well and you can make the changes."

You can manage your recommendations as well. You can edit or withdraw ones you have sent, request revisions and hide recommendations through clicking recommendations and then manage at the bottom of your profile.

LinkedIn & Social Selling For Business Development

Example

Recommendation from Simon Elliot, Director of Business Development at ARAMARK

Simon Elliot
Inspiring Life at Work - International Food & Facilities Management

> My business focus leads me to dealing with complex sales with long sales cycles where relationships really matter. I find LinkedIn a very valuable tool to build my network, keep in touch, communicate and keep in constant contact with those relationships.
>
> I attended one of Brynne's sessions - LinkedIn & Social Selling for Business Development - Given that I have been using LinkedIn for so long, I wasn't expecting to learn too much but I was wrong - I learned powerful strategies on how to leverage my existing network that I was completely under utilizing. The techniques were easy to implement and I saw results very quickly.
>
> Whether you are a beginner at LinkedIn or a power user, I highly recommend that you take Brynne's class - LinkedIn & Social Selling for Business Development - I believe that she also has a book coming out on Amazon which I am sure will make for very interesting read. **less**

Publications

If you're a published author, guest blogger or have online whitepapers, publications is a fantastic way to get that message out. If you have a book on Amazon or any other site, the link will take them there. If you don't have a published book, use publications as a fantastic lead generation tool. That means that your website or email services can offer opt-in forms for people to download your content. That simply means, you take them to a page, they fill out the information you requested and they get your white paper. Easy – and effective. This is social selling.

 Make sure your white paper isn't selling your product or service. It needs to be a thought leadership piece that your reader gains value from having read it. You can burn a prospect very quickly if they feel like they've been duped. Remember they paid for your content through offering up their contact information – respect that. Now, be sure that your logo, phone number and website address is all over the whitepaper, so when it is time for them to call you – you have made it easy! You can also have a call to action to either download another white paper, contact you for a consultation or watch educational videos living on your website.

33 Social Selling Tips from Leading Social Selling Leaders
August 2014

▸ 32 team members, including:

 Brynne Tillman
Transforming the Way Professionals Gr...

 Koka Sexton
Transforming the way companies do bu...

 Alex Hisaka
Content Marketing Manager at LinkedIn

 Jill Rowley
Keynote Speaker ** Social Selling Evan...

Duplicate Accounts

You may discover you have more than one LinkedIn account. If you get a message that says the email address you're attempting to use is already associated with another account, this means that you probably have another LinkedIn account using that email address. To fix this problem, once you have identified all of your accounts you will either merge them into the account you wish to keep or close the one(s) you don't want. If you close an account, after 48 hours, you are able to add the email address from the closed account to the one you kept open.

How to find and CLOSE a duplicate account:

1. Find your other account(s) by searching your name in the people search box and click the magnify glass. The profile with the You icon is the account where you're currently signed in. A profile containing your information that doesn't have a You icon is a duplicate account.

2. Sign in to the account you want to close. If you can't remember your password, click the Forgot Password? link. If you don't have access to the email associated with the account see "contact LinkedIn below" If you are deleting the account make a note of any connections that are missing from the account you plan to keep so you can re-invite them from your other account.

3. IMPORTANT: Make sure you're in the account YOU WANT TO CLOSE

    1. Hover over your name on the top right of your account
    2. Click Settings
    3. Choose the Account tab on the bottom left
    4. Click Close Account

4. If you can't log into an old account visit http://help.linkedin.com

    1. Copy the URL for the account you wish to delete
    2. Type duplicate accounts and enter
    3. Click contact us up top
    4. Send a message request to merge accounts with the following information:

Hello, I currently have 2 LinkedIn accounts. The one I am sending this message from is the one I wish to keep. I would like to request that you delete http://www.linkedin.com/pub/abc123. The email that is associated with the old account is myoldemail@notvalid.com and my name on the account is My Name (you don't need to log into the email, you just need to know it). If you don't know the email, they may ask you some security questions.

If you can log into your old account, you may want to export your connections and then import them into your primary account.

LinkedIn & Social Selling For Business Development

Privacy Settings

You do have some controls over what others see when they visit your profile. It is in Settings where you determine these settings. This is different than your Public Profile settings. We recommend you look through all of your options and choose exactly how you want to be represented on LinkedIn.

1.   Hover over your little picture on the top right.
2.   Click on Privacy and Settings review.
3.   Enter your password.

From here visit the many sections where you can manage your account:

1.   On the top left you can add, edit or remove your emails as well as choose which email you would like to make your primary or default email for your LinkedIn messages. Note: in each of your individual groups you can choose any email you have listed to be your default email for messages.
2.   Change your password.
3.   Confirm your subscription level and features that you receive as well as compare to other paid account benefits.
4.   Privacy settings will help you turn your activity broadcasts, your activity feed preferences, what others see when you look at them (if you are in stalking mode, simply turn this to anonymous, troll away and turn it back on when you are done. No one will be the wiser. If you forget to turn it back to full view, you will not be able to see who has viewed your profile, so don't forget to reset your settings!)

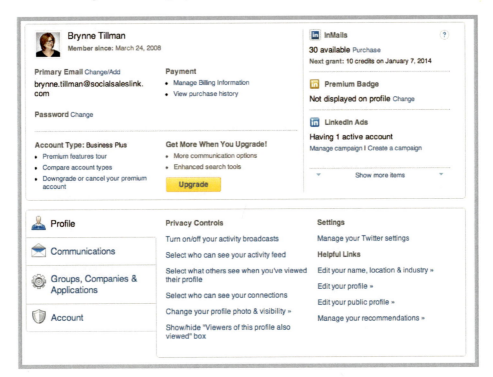

31

Company Page

Create Your Company Page

A Company Page helps others learn more about your company's job opportunities, work culture, products, and services. You can create one from clicking on Company Tab and then click on Add Company on the top right of the screen. You must have an official company email. Gmail or others like it will not be accepted.

To add a Company Page follow these steps:

1. Hover over Interest and click Companies.
2. Click the Add a Company link in the upper right area of the page.
3. Enter your company's official name and your work email address.
4. Add designated admins by typing in their names and selecting them from the drop-down.
They must be a first connection.
5. Add a banner image (PNG, JPEG, or GIF; max size 2 MB. Image must be 646 x 220 pixels or larger).
6. Add a standard logo and a small logo and company specialities.
7. If you run a LinkedIn group or have one that your company promotes, you may add that to featured groups on your company profile.
8. Include a company description (often you can copy this from your current website).
9. Add Location, years in business, type of business, website and phone number.
10. Save.

If you already have a company page, click the Edit box and you can click on the arrow to add products or services. If you don't have this button, you can identify who is the assigned administrator by clicking See Admin List and you can view the owners and Managers that are able to grant you permission.

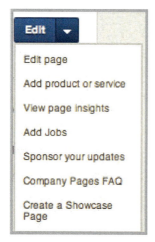

LinkedIn & Social Selling For Business Development

Add Content to Your Company Page

Adding products and/or services is important in branding your offerings. It is simple to do and has a big impact. If you're the administrator of your Company Page, you can add information for up to 25 products and services. If you have the edit button then you have administrative permission. If you do not, check the bottom right hand section of the company home page to identify who the current admin is and they can grant you permission to do the edits. The next steps are how to build out your company page.

1. Go to your Company Page and click the Products & Services tab.
2. Move your cursor over Edit in the upper right and click Add product or service.
3. Click Get started.
4. Choose Product or Service.
5. Select a category from the drop-down menu.
6. Name your Product or Services.
7. Add an image and description and key features.
8. Add Website.
9. Designate a contact person by typing in their name.
10. Add a promotion or discount for the product or services.
11. If you have a video on YouTube, add a link here.
12. Click Publish on the top right.
13. The first product you list on your Products & Services page will be spotlighted in the Products & Services module.
14. You can switch the order of how your products and services appear in edit mode.

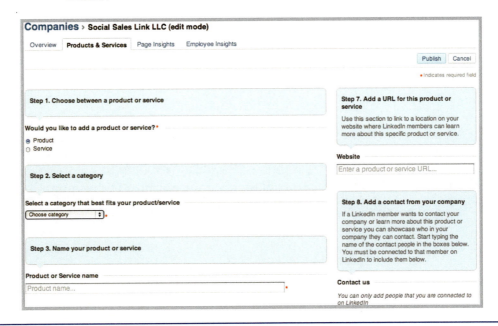

Company Banner

Above your products and services lives a 3 banner scroll that can help drive traffic to your website.

1. Products and Services
2. Edit
3. Keep page in its current version in step 1
4. Describe your company in a compelling way
5. Add a YouTube Video URL Link
6. Add 3 images and be sure they have a call to action that encourages visitors to click through. Images must be a PNG, JPEG or GIF max size 2 MB and sized to fit 646 X 222 pixels.
7. Add URL that coincides with your message

 You can easily create an image in PowerPoint, right click it and save as a JPEG on your desktop. Open the image in Paint or Preview and resize accordingly. Be sure to add your contact information on your banner. Remember, if the objective is to get engagement, make it easy for them to contact you!

Showcase Pages

Showcase pages allow you to describe and promote your Company Page through dedicated sub-pages or "child-pages" for many aspects of your business offerings. Interested members can now follow each Showcase Page just as they follow your Company Page.

Showcase Pages were developed for nurturing relationships with interested parties who want to follow specific products, services, initiatives, projects and or offerings of your business, and not for marketing campaigns and promotions. Showcase pages need to be managed and developed, unlike a static Company Page, so before you take it on, be sure to have a plan in place!

The following guidelines have been provided by LinkedIn:
First, please review the required specifications for creating a Showcase Page. Requirement and specifications:

You must be a Company Page administrator in order to create a Showcase Page. Learn more about becoming a Company Page admin. Other information you'll need:

1. Showcase Page name
2. Showcase Page description (75-200 characters)
3. Industry
4. Name of at least 1 Showcase Page administrator
5. Hero Image (recommended)
6. Learn more about the specifications for the elements of a Showcase Page.

If you're an admin of the parent Company Page, here's how you can create a child Showcase Page:

1. Click the down arrow next to the blue Edit button on the Company Page
2. Select Create a Showcase Page.
3. Enter a page name and assign administrators for the Showcase Page.
4. You must be a 1st degree connection to assign someone as an administrator.
5. Click Create.
6. The page exists and can be edited at this point, but won't appear in search or in the linked pages shown for your Company Page yet.

Either you or the administrators you've assigned can finalize the page details, and then click Publish to make it public.
To get back to your Showcase page, you can search for it from the top of any LinkedIn Page or go to your parent Company Page and select the Showcase page in the page tree along the right rail.

Note: You can create up to 10 Showcase Pages through your Company Page.

Showcase Page element specifications:

Hero Image: Minimum 974 x 330 pixels. PNG, JPEG, or GIF. Maximum file size 2 MB. You can crop your image once it's uploaded.
Logo: 100 x 60 pixels. Image will be resized to fit.
Square logo: 50 x 50 pixels. Image will be resized to fit.

Post to Company Page

Just like posting to your newsfeed, you have the ability to post articles and links to your company page. You need to be a designated admin in order to post. Each time you post an article it will appear in the newsfeed of your company page followers. We recommend that you post blogs, press releases, upcoming events, and all other pertinent links to get the most exposure. You also have the option to share it will all of your followers or your targeted audience.

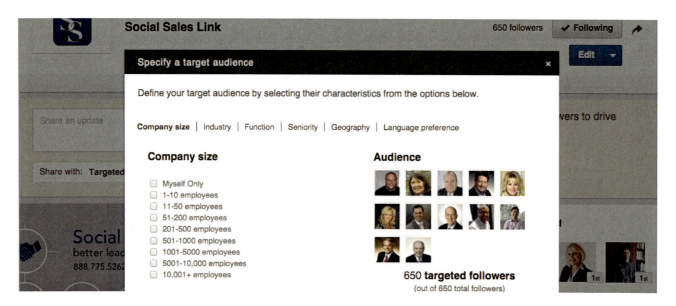

Everyone that has admin permission will be able to view how many followers not only saw the post, but engaged with the post through likes and comments.

LinkedIn gives you the ability to upload a PDF, document, PowerPoint or other files that is then available for your followers to view. From the update status box, simply click the paperclip. Be sure to edit the title and add a description.

LinkedIn & Social Selling For Business Development

Company Analytics

If you're a page administrator, you can view analytical data about your Company Page or Showcase page. The analytics page helps you gain deeper insights into your page performance by:

1. Seeing how engaging your individual posts are
2. Identifying trends across key metrics
3. Understanding more about your follower demographics and sources
4. Understanding more about your page traffic and activity

To see Company Page analytics, you must be a Company Page administrator. To see Company Page analytics:

1. Go to your Company Page.
2. Click the Analytics tab at the top of the page.

To see Showcase Page analytics, you must be a Showcase Page administrator. To see the Showcase Page analytics:

1. From Company Page and scroll down to the Other pages section on the right side of the page.
2. Click the Showcase Page you'd like to review.
3. Click the down arrow icon next to the blue Edit button in the top right.
4. Select View Analytics from the list.

Showcase Page analytics are not combined with the analytics of the Company Page.

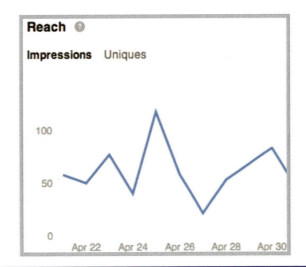

LinkedIn Publishing

LinkedIn Blogging 101

There is a lot of good content getting published on LinkedIn, but not only that, if done correctly, lots of people are viewing it, liking it and commenting! This is one of the best ways to brand you and your company as the thought leader and subject matter expert in your industry.

And guess what...it is really simple to do. Here are the steps to publishing a blog post on LinkedIn:

1. Click on your home page.

2. Click on the pencil icon in the update status box.

3. Click on Add an Image (recommended size 689x400 pixels).

4. Type in your title.

5. Write your blog or paste it from a document.

6. To hyperlink a word or phrase highlight it click on the link icon on the toolbar above, paste your destination link and click submit.

7. To bring in an image or video click on the camera, upload the file and Submit.

8. Click on image and drag on corner to resize.

9. Add a link to the image as well.

10. Click Save to save as a draft or Publish to go live.

One of the great benefits of publishing on LinkedIn is that all of your connections and followers will get notified in the little gray flag on the top right of their profile that you have posted a new publication with the title (one of the reasons why the title is critical, it is what will pull them in).

> " *Consider using different fonts (H1 or H2), **bold**, italic, <u>underline</u> and quote options to draw the eye in and improve the reader experience.*

LinkedIn & Social Selling For Business Development

A Dozen Dos and Don'ts of LinkedIn Publications

LinkedIn Publications is the best new social selling tool for anyone in a sales role. The key, however, is to use it well and the way it was designed to be used, as a content machine.

Thought leadership is about educating the reader and is the key to gaining trust, attracting your target market and developing relationships. As this rolls out to 300m LinkedIn members, it is very important to use this powerful tool correctly, so here are Social Sales Link's Dos and Don'ts for **EVERY** LinkedIn publication:

1. **Do** educate. Make sure everything you share has value to the reader.

2. **Don't** promote or advertise any products, promotions, paid seminars or webinars or any other offering as your primary message.

3. **Do** offer a take-away, something the reader can implement even if they don't work with you.

4. **Don't** make the only take-away be that they have to contact or hire you to learn how.

5. **Do** have a call to action that is in-line with your content. A call to action can be anything from a download, watch a video with lead capture, and schedule a free consultation.

6. **Don't** make the call to action part of your primary message, it is only appropriate when it is additional value to what you have already provided to the reader.

7. **Do** make the information clear and concise.

8. **Don't** make the content longer than a 3 minute read...they stop anyway.

9. **Do** respect the boundaries of social selling.

10. **Don't** cross the line and become a self promoter, you will create what you fear the most, a bad reputation.

11. **Do** be honest and authentic in your approach.

12. **Don't** do nothing, your voice, your message, your expertise is why people will engage with you, and silence gets you silence. Put your best foot forward and share your valuable insights. You will be seen as a thought leader and a subject matter expert.

7 Key Elements to a Successful LinkedIn Publication Blog Post

As a follow up to last week's blog post LinkedIn Publications Dos and Don'ts I wanted to share the 7 Elements that are necessary for your blog post to really be successful.

By now you should have the ability to publish a blog post on LinkedIn, which, by the way, is the coolest new tool you have in your social selling tool box. (From your home page click on the pencil in update status box to begin blogging)

The key to being seen as a thought leader and your industry's expert is the creation and publication of your own original content. You no longer have to start a whole new blog site, be at the mercy of your web developer or wait until your company posts a piece worth sharing…you now have control over your own brand and reputation! Social Sales Link believes there are 7 elements that are absolutely necessary to a post's success:

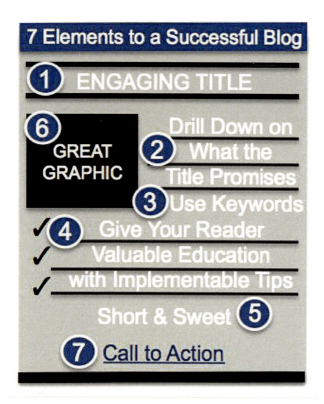

1. It needs to have a **catchy title** that engages your reader and tells them what they are going to learn.

2. You have to **deliver on the promise**, don't bait and switch, and be sure the content matches the title.

3. Be sure to **include keywords** that your reader would use when searching for content related to you content to maximize Search Engine Optimized (SEO).

4. Give them an **implementable take-away**. Be sure that they leave with more than just ideas but a strategy or tactic.

5. Keep the reading time **under 3 minutes**, they stop reading anyway.

6. Include **a powerful graphic** that is clear, tells the post's story and attracts the readers' eye.

7. Be sure to have a **call to action**, a next step that you would like you reader to do.

Calls to Action

1. **LOW RISK** – <u>CLICK HERE</u> to watch 5 LinkedIn Tips so You Never have to Cold Call Again OR <u>CLICK HERE</u> to download 11 LinkedIn Tips for Sales Professionals

2. **MEDIUM RISK** - <u>CLICK HERE</u> to schedule a FREE consultation or a time to talk.

3. **HIGH RISK** – <u>CLICK HERE</u> to purchase our LinkedIn & Social Selling Book on Amazon. Or <u>CLICK HERE</u> to Register for a class.

Share Publications in Groups

You can share your publication in all of your groups and with targeted connections with a couple of quick steps.

1. Click on your profile.
2. Click on the title of your post.
3. Click on the LinkedIn Share Button above your content.
4. Click post to groups.
5. Type in title of your post.
6. Add a teaser in the description.
7. Start typing the name of your groups beginning with the letter "A".
8. Select groups from the dropdown (you can add all of your groups here and share at the same time).
9. Click Share.
10. You can also send the link with a message to targeted individuals by typing in their name in "send to individuals". Be sure to customize the message. If you send to more than one connection, be sure to uncheck the "allow recipients to see each others' names and emails".

WARNING: Be sure the groups you are posting in are open to your content. You don't want to get SWAM'd (site wide automated moderation). If you get flagged for breaking the group rules or posting inappropriate content, you will be moderated in every group and future posts may not be published. Know the rules of the groups, and if you have any questions always message the group owner before posting.

50 Blog Title Ideas

90% of why people click through to your post is because your title intrigued them. Yup, it really doesn't matter how good your content is if your headline is engaging. That being said, your content is what will build your long term followers and your reputation, so if you don't want to be a 1 hit wonder, your content does need to live up to your blog title's promise. The biggest challenge I tend to hear when it comes to blogging on LinkedIn is "I just don't know where to start". So here are 101 title ideas that can inspire you and that you can adapt to your product, service or industry when you hit a writer's block. Keep in mind at all times, does your prospective client care about the topic you are writing on. Be sure it is client centric blogging not competitor centric blogging. So even though you may see (Your Industry) many times throughout this post, keep in mind that may be interchangeable with your clients industry as well.

1. A Little Mistake that Cost a XXX - XXX.
2. 5 Tips on How to Win Friends and Influence People (IN YOUR INDUSTRY)
3. 7 Steps to Making More Money Doing Less Work (IN YOUR INDUSTRY)
4. 3 Ways to Increase Your Revenue 3X in 3 Weeks (IN YOUR INDUSTRY)
5. 10 Things to Add to Your To Do List if You are XXX
6. Why People Dumber Than You Get Promoted Faster (IN YOUR INDUSTRY)
7. How You Can Do Anything You want Even Better Than You are Now (IN YOUR INDUSTRY)
8. How to Turn Your Great Idea into a Profitable One (IN YOUR INDUSTRY)
9. If You Knew Then What You Do Now (ABOUT YOUR INDUSTRY) What Would You Have Done Differently?
10. Warning Don't Ever Do XXX
11. To Boldly Go Where No One has Gone Before (IN YOUR INDUSTRY)
12. Why XXX is the Most Important Step (IN YOUR INDUSTRY)
13. How to Get More High Fives From Your Boss, Shareholders and Clients (IN YOUR INDUSTRY)
14. Can You Pass this Test (IN YOUR INDUSTRY)
15. 5 Steps to Influencing Your Boss's Decisions (IN YOUR INDUSTRY)
16. 10 Steps to Never Cold Call Again (IN YOUR INDUSTRY)
17. What Your Customers Aren't Telling You (IN YOUR INDUSTRY)
18. They Just Don't Get it (IN YOUR INDUSTRY) Do You?
19. What Motivates You to Succeed? Is it Working?
20. XXX in 5 Minutes a Day
21. The #1 Secret Your Competition Doesn't Want You to Know
22. 7 Ways to Negotiate Even Better (IN YOUR INDUSTRY)
23. Small Step for Man, Giant Leap for (YOUR INDUSTRY)

24. How Many Ingredients is in Your Secret Sauce (IN YOUR INDUSTRY)
25. What Happens in (Your Company), Stays in (Your Company)
26. Top 10 (YOUR INDUSTRY) Trending Topics
27. The Top 7 Skills Your Decision Maker Wants to See (IN YOUR INDUSTRY)
28. What I Wish I Knew Before I Launched My Company
29. 5 Things You Don't Know About Your Prospect
30. 7 Things You Need to Know About Your Prospect
31. 9 Things You Don't Know About Your Competition
32. 11 Resources that Give You a Competitive Edge (IN YOUR INDUSTRY)
33. What Successful People in Your Industry Don't Want You to Know
34. The Top Mistakes in Your Industry
35. What to Expect Next Year in Your Industry
36. The Essential Checklist to XXX
37. 10 Simple Things You Can Do Today to be Productive
38. Stop Drop and Roll – Your Pants are on Fire (CRISIS MANAGEMENT IN YOUR INDUSTRY)
39. 3 Tips that Will Get You on Page 1 of Google
40. 7 Writing Tactics You are Wasting Your Time On
41. 21 Resources that Will Make You a Master (YOUR INDUSTRY)
42. Top 5 Habits of Successful Entrepreneurs in (YOUR INDUSTRY_
43. 9 Secrets for Awesome Blog Posts (IN YOUR INDUSTRY)
44. Give Me Freedom or Give Me Cash (IN YOUR INDUSTRY)
45. Warning Do This Right Now (IN YOUR INDUSTRY)
46. Here is the #1 Method that 1000s are Using to be Successful (IN YOUR INDUSTRY)
47. Now You Can Have the Job of Your Dreams
48. Life, Liberty and Pursuit of Happiness - It is Your Right, Go Do It!
49. What Everyone in Your Industry Forgets to Do
50. When it is Time to Break Up with Your Vendor?

BONUS: Every time you answer a client question, speak about what you do or come up with a great idea, that is a blog topic. If you are more of a talker than a writer, start recording your ideas on your SMART phone and have them transcribed. Blogging is an easy way to brand yourself as a thought leader and the subject matter expert.

Your Home Page

Share Updates

So many fabulous opportunities are waiting for us every day on our home page. We are going to start with the obvious- Share an Update. Much like Facebook, this is your opportunity to share what is going on in your world. But keep it brief and keep it professional. Honestly, no one really cares where you are going for lunch, unless you're Brad Pitt! So when you post, think about what the readers want to see. Maybe it is new product information or a news article on your industry. The purpose of these updates is twofold: Firstly, to establish you as a thought leader and subject matter expert in your area. Secondly, to drive traffic to your website, email and phone. Rule of thumb: ONE self-promoting post for every five you put out there. If you spam your promotions we promise, people will stop reading your "stuff", so don't do it!

Content you can share:

1. Original content that lives on your website as a blog. This is the best content to share as it will get your readers to your website where they can learn even more about you and your offerings. If you do post blogs, we recommend having a call to action at the bottom of every post. It could be a low risk offer, like download a white paper, a medium risk (such as a free webinar or 30 minute consultation) or a higher risk (such as register for a paid event or service.)

2. Discussions or questions that you can post without a link (however these need to be in the group itself as you cannot share an update from your home page if it doesn't have a link).

3. Polls (we will get to this in more detail in the Groups section).

4. Other peoples' content such as blogs and news articles. If you go this route we highly recommend that you add commentary, your perspective or reason for sharing.

LinkedIn & Social Selling For Business Development

Navigating Your Home Page

The "Who's Viewed Your Profile" feature allows you to see who's been looking at your profile recently and how many times you have shown up in search results. With the free LinkedIn account you can see the last 5 viewers. If you upgrade your account you can see everyone who has looked at your account in the last 90 days. However, if the viewer has limited their settings you may not see any of the information.

Who's Viewed Your Profile

29 Your profile has been viewed by 29 people in the past 1 day.

21 You have shown up in search results 21 times in the past 3 days.

1. You can select what others see when you've viewed their profile from the Settings page.
2. There are three different ways we show info on who's viewed your profile, based on the profile viewer's privacy settings:
- Name and headline.
- Anonymous profile characteristics such as industry and title.
- Anonymous LinkedIn user.

As we mentioned, with the free LinkedIn account, you are able to see a list of the last 5 viewers of your profile. If there is someone that it makes sense to have a discussion with and they are a 1st connection, reach out with a quick note:

Hello XXX,

Thank you for visiting my profile, I had a chance to look at yours and I think it might make sense for us to have a phone call. I have next Monday morning and Thursday afternoon available; does either of these times work for you?

You may notice on the sample to the left that the second viewer down just says "LinkedIn member," this is because that particular person has chosen to go completely incognito. They have changed their settings (we call it stalker mode). This allows them to look at other profiles without anyone knowing. The downside is if you have a free profile and you choose this mode you are unable to see the people who have searched your profile as well. Essentially, LinkedIn sees this as a pay to play.

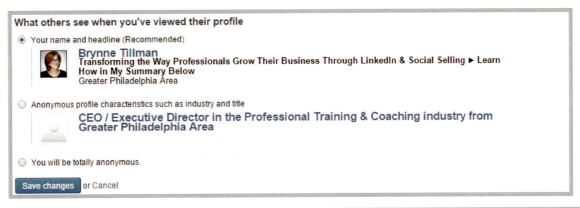

Did you ever check someone out then three clicks later you try to go back but, you just can't find them? 'Recently Viewed' can solve that problem.

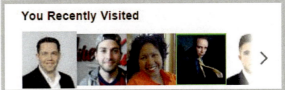

51

Navigating Continued

Beth Rosenfeld, a sales trainer, makes a habit of checking out "WHO'S VIEWED YOUR PROFILE?" on LinkedIn. One day she noticed a Sales Director from a well-known (Ernst & Young Award Winning) Philadelphia based company, had checked her out. Knowing that this company was a great prospect she sent him an invitation to connect on LinkedIn. Along with the invitation was a personal note stating: "Thanks for checking out my profile. After looking at your profile, it appears that we have some contacts and Business Development efforts in common. Should you have any interest in exploring how we might be able to help one another in 2013, I would love to have a conversation with you. Please feel free to contact me. Hope to hear from you soon".

Long story short, he reached out to her, and ended up introducing her to the decision makers within his company. Beth scheduled an appointment to talk with them about our company's services and subsequently, this company became a client!

It is always fun to see our connections and a snapshot of our network. Everything your connections are posting and doing will come up in your feed. If you are looking to filter the information, click on All Updates and choose the specific information you are looking to see. We recommend that you spend some time in the Connections filter (this is where you can identify new connections that your connections have just made). This is a great opportunity to leverage your network to meet new people.

LinkedIn will often recommend groups based on your profile and other groups you belong to. Joining groups on LinkedIn is one of the best ways to engage people you would have not have otherwise met. Groups typically have a specific purpose and attract specific people, and LinkedIn will try and match groups to you based on your profile. This shows up on the right hand side of your homepage. You can click through to see more suggested groups. If you have ideas that you want to share with the LinkedIn staff, you can also do so by clicking "Feedback".

Ever wonder how many impressions your posts are really getting? Now you can!

LinkedIn & Social Selling For Business Development

People You May Know

If you are looking to grow your network, LinkedIn will recommend People You May Know based on your profile information, common connections and industry. Every once in a while we find someone that is an old colleague or classmate whom we are thrilled to reach out to and reconnect. This is an area to check out occasionally. Click "See More" at the bottom to get a continuous list of potential connections. Be sure to add a personal message to each new invitation to connect.

Navigating Pulse

LinkedIn Pulse is your source for professional news tailored to you. It's the place to discover compelling content and discuss what's trending with millions of professionals worldwide. Available on LinkedIn.com, Android, and iOS, Pulse allows you to read and share your news from any location.

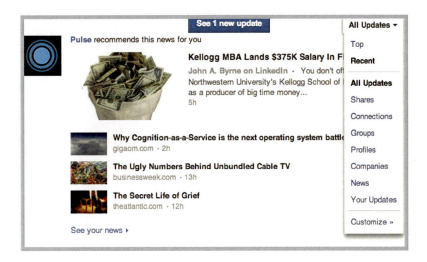

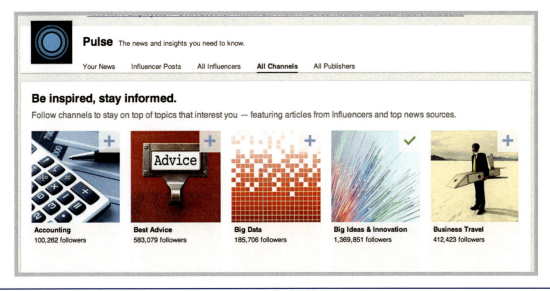

Your Connections

Who Should I Connect With?

SSL looks at a connection request as if someone called your office and left a message. If you would return that call, you should respond to the request. You don't have to accept necessarily, you can reply without accepting. Just click on the arrow down next to the accept button.

We teach LinkedIn as a warm market tool. Our rule of thumb is to connect with folks that you can ask for introductions. If it happens to be someone that you don't know but is a:

1. A potential prospect.
2. Strategic alliance, center of influence or referral source.
3. Possible introduction for one of your connections.

Don't just accept invitation, engage with them. Send a note thanking them for connecting with you and a call to action.

Thank you for connecting with me on LinkedIn. As a networker, I always like to start off a new relationship in giving mode. I want to share with you one of our videos - Leveraging LinkedIn for Business Development so You Never Have to Cold Call Again! http://bit.ly/SSLLinkedInVideoTips - let me know if you find this helpful.

Good Networking,
Brynne

P.S. I will also add you to my LinkedIn email tips - so please look for those!

OR

Thank you for connecting with me on LinkedIn. Typically I like to have a call with my new connections so we can explore ways we might be able to help each other out. I have Monday morning and Thursday afternoon available for a call, let me know what works best for you.

Good Networking,
Brynne

P.S. I will also add you to my LinkedIn email tips - so please look for those!

We always let new connections know that we are adding them to an email list, this way when we export them we already have informed them that they will be added to our respective Constant Contact email databases. We recommend having the first message sent to them with an opt-out as well to avoid spamming our connections.

LinkedIn & Social Selling For Business Development

Inviting Connections

You can ask someone to join your professional LinkedIn network by sending them an invitation to connect. Once they accept your invitation, they become your 1st-degree connection. We recommend that you send invitations to people you know because 1st-degree connections are given access to the primary email address on your account and visibility into your connections.

You can invite people to connect from the following areas:

Finding a member's profile - Click the Connect button on their profile page.

1. In the search box at the top of your profile click the icon on the left and choose people.
2. Type the name of the person you are trying to find.
3. If they come up in the drop down select the name.
4. If there are multiple people with that name, then click the magnify glass and you will be taken to a list where there are more choices.
5. Click through the profile.
6. Click connect on the profile and add a personal message.

To invite people using their email address:

1. Click the Add Connections icon in the top right of your LinkedIn homepage.
2. Click the Any Email icon (looks like an envelope).
3. Click the Invite by Individual email link found under More Ways to Connect.
4. Type the email addresses, separating them with commas.
5. Click Send Invitations.
6. WARNING: You cannot customize invitations that are sent this way.

Personal Note

The purpose of LinkedIn is to get engagement, so if you connect with new people be sure to do more than "accept".

Dear XXX,
Thank you for your connection on LinkedIn. Typically, I like to have a conversation with new people in my network so we can explore how we might be able to help each other. I have Monday morning and Thursday afternoon available for a call, what works best for you?

Looking forward to speaking with you,

Brynne Tillman

Don't Connect & Forget!

There are many sins that people commit on LinkedIn. This one is by far the most common sin and if you are in a sales or business development role you want to be sure you never commit it.

You work all day to connect with new people, have conversations and get appointments, but often miss the lowest hanging fruit.

When someone invites you to connect on LinkedIn it is as they called and left you a voicemail. Take advantage of this opportunity and convert the right ones to brief phone calls or at minimum start an email dialogue.

Here is what to do with people that invite you to connect:

1. Click through to their profile and determine if you want to accept or ignore their invitation (best practices is if you ignore don't mark "I don't know" or "SPAM" unless you really feel it is obtrusive as it will affect them negatively). Treat them as if they were at a networking meeting with you. If you would want to have a conversation, you will want to engage on LinkedIn. Evaluate if they are a potential prospect, strategic alliance, center of influence or simply someone that others in your network would want to know.

2. If you accept, decide if you wish to have a phone call or begin an email correspondence.

Phone calls for prospects or strategic alliances: Dear XXX, It is nice to be connected on LinkedIn. Typically I like to have a brief conversation with my new connections so we can explore ways we might be able to work or network together. Here is a link to my calendar http://scheduleacallwithbrynne.com/ please pick a time that works best for you.

Someone you would like in your network but don't want a phone call at this time. XXX, welcome to my network. Typically I like to learn more about my connections and share a bit about me so we can determine how we can be of value to each others' network. I am a Social Selling and LinkedIn trainer that works with Fortune 1000 VP of Sales to bring their team strategies and tactics so they can build their pipeline, reduce their sales cycle and close more business. Please share with me who you work with and the value you bring.

If you are on the fence, consider the "Reply Don't Accept Yet" option. Simply click on the Inbox, choose Invitations on the left hand side, click the down arrow next to the accept button and send a message. XXX, thank you for your invitation to connect on LinkedIn. Typically I only connect with professionals I know, please share with me how you came across my profile and how you think we can help each other out. I am looking forward to hearing from you.

BONUS: When you invite someone to connect and you receive an email that says "Hannah Gordon has accepted your connection request" you want to be sure respond accordingly. Determine why you reached out in the first place, is she a prospect, referral source or simply someone you wish to be connected to but not sure if it warrants a conversation yet. Then, send a similar message as above.

RESOURCE: My prospecting and strategic alliance conversations have increased significantly since I began using TimeTrade as it syncs in real-time with my calendar and others can pick a time to talk that works best for them.

I purchased a domain name - http://scheduleacallwithbrynne.com, created a landing page on my website (that drives traffic) and offer 15 minute or 30 minute time slots. They click through and pick the best available time for them, it instantly populates my calendar and I receive an email notification. No more dropped opportunities because it took too long to find a mutually beneficial time to talk.

TimeTrade will give you a generic link that you can use or you can purchase a vanity URL on GoDaddy and redirect it to your TimeTrade account. Offer it to everyone you would like to speak with and watch your appointments skyrocket!

@Mentions to Prospect

Using the @mention feature on LinkedIn is a great way to get your connections to read and engage with your updates and comments. LinkedIn gives us the ability to @mention individuals and companies. When you mention a person, their profile will be LinkedIn publicly to the post, and if you @mention a company, the update will be linked to their LinkedIn Company Page from your update or comment. @Mentions will notify your connections or company that you're talking about them.

- There are 2 places to @mention a connection or company. First, from your homepage's update box and Second, click comment on someone else's update.
- Type "@" and then type a name in the box. A drop down list of potential people or companies will appear and you can choose one to @mention.
- To @mention individuals in a LinkedIn update, you must be connected to them directly. The one exception is, if you are engaging via comments in any update that they have contributed to, you can mention them in that feed. You can @mention all companies.

Here is how to use the @mentions strategically:

- Share your prospect's content in your update and @mention EXAMPLE: Must Read - Are you being SPAMMED on LinkedInhttp://sslink.co/SpamonLinkedIn by @Michael de Groot
- If you publish or find content, @mention your prospect in the updateEXAMPLE: As someone that publishes great content on @LinkedIn, I thought this blog, Who Owns Your Content on LinkedIn http://sslink.co/WhoOwnsYourLinkedInContent would be of interest @Cory Glabraith"
- Quote an influencer on LinkedIn and @mention them - this will get visibility from the influencer as well as their audience. Be sure you don't spam here, if you over use it with the same influencer it can back fire. EXAMPLE: Brilliant seminar today with @Pat Walsh, he talked about how to bridge the gap between sales and marketing!
- If you read about awards your prospects or clients have received or mentions in the news, congratulate them in a LinkedIn update. EXAMPLE:Congratulations @CETRA Language Solutions on making the Philadelphia 100 list!

Withdrawing an Invitation

In many cases, you can withdraw an invitation if the recipient hasn't taken any action.

1. Click Inbox at the top of your home page.
2. Click Sent on the left.
3. Click the Sent Invitations tab under the top navigational bar.
4. Find an invitation without "Accepted" by the name. (If it has already been accepted you will have to remove the connection, not withdraw it)
5. Click Delete.

The recipient will not be notified about a withdrawn invitation.

This is a great way to quickly look through your outstanding invitations. It gives you a list of people to recontact.

Importing

To import your address book from Yahoo, Gmail, Hotmail, AOL and other webmail providers:

1. From the Contacts Tab select Add Connections.
2. Enter your email address (and password if prompted) then click Continue.

Clicking on the box above the first contact will unselect everyone on the "Imported Contacts" list so that invitations aren't sent.

Exporting

We recommend that LinkedIn users export their connections monthly. To export your connections:

1. Hover over Network at the top of your homepage and select Contacts.
2. Click the Settings icon near the top right.
3. Under Advanced Settings on the right, click Export LinkedIn Connections.
4. Enter the security text if prompted.
5. Click Export and save the file in a location where it can be found easily.

Although many categories will appear on your spreadsheet, only the first name, last name, email address, current company (if they have 2 current companies the first one will be listed), and job descriptions are exported.

Taking Notes

You can add notes for anyone who's saved in your LinkedIn Contacts.

1. Visit your connections profile.
2. Click Relationship in the top section of the profile.
3. Click Note.
4. Type your note into the field.
5. Click Save.
6. Your note will be date stamped and saved in the Relationship section of the profile and will only be visible to you.

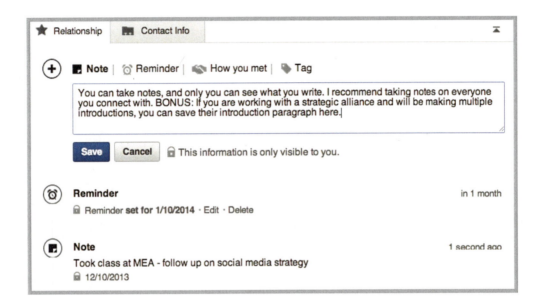

Reminder

You can set a reminder for anyone who is saved in your LinkedIn Contacts.

1. When you are on a profile Click Relationship.
2. Click Reminder.
3. Type the reason for the reminder and save.

Your reminder will be sent via a daily LinkedIn Contacts email. It will also appear at the top of your Contacts page as an item pending completion.

Tagging

Tagging is a very powerful marketing tool. You can tag or untag anyone who's saved in your LinkedIn Contacts. Tags are categories to help organize and sort your contacts for searches and messaging. They can be added from the Contacts page or a person's profile.

We recommend that you have no more than 50 contacts per tag, as that is the maximum number you can message at one time. If you reach 50, then create a second tag for that category, i.e. Managers | Managers1.

To add or remove a tag on a profile:

1. Go to your connections profile and click Relationship in the top section of the profile under the member's photo.
2. Click Tag.
3. Check the box next to an existing tag.
4. To create a new category, click +Add new tag, type in the name and click Save.
5. To remove a tag, uncheck the box next to it.

To add or remove a tag from the Contacts page:

1. Hover over Network at the top of your homepage and click Contacts.
2. Hover over the contact in the list and click Tag below the contact's information.
3. Check the box next to an existing tag or click +Add new tag to create a new one.
4. The tag will be visible to you on the person's contact information and on their profile. You can click the tag in these areas to see all other profiles with the same tag.

Only you will see the tags you've created.
You can create up to 200 new and unique tags or delete old ones.

Messaging Tagged Contacts

1. Hover over Network at the top of your homepage and click Contacts.
2. Click Filter by and click on Tag.
3. Choose a category and all your tagged connections will be listed.
4. To send a message, check select all.
5. Click message.
6. Be sure to uncheck Allow recipients to see each other's names and email address to blind copy the message.

Sort & Filter Connections

LinkedIn's new look has brought some great new features. It is very simple to sort and filter your connections based on some key criteria.

To sort your Contacts click on connections at the top of your homepage.
Click Sort by above your list of Contacts to reveal the following sorting options:

- Recent Conversation - Sort in order of contacts most recently corresponded with at the top. This is the default setting.
- First Name - Sort by first name
- Last Name - Sort by last name
- New - Sorted with the contacts most recently synced to your account at the top.

To filter your Contacts click Filter by above your list of contacts to reveal the following filter options:

- All Contacts - Includes LinkedIn connections and contacts synced from other sources.
- Connections Only - Your LinkedIn connections only, excludes synced contacts
- Company - Visually group contacts by company name. Click a company name to see individual contacts.
- Tag - Filter by individual tags you've created. Click a tag to see individual contacts that have that tag. If you had Profile Organizer, those folders are now tags.
- Location - Visually group contacts by city name. Click a city name to see individual contacts.
- Title - Visually group contacts by current title. Click a title to see individual contacts.
- Sources - View contacts by imported source.
- Saved - All contacts whose profiles you saved on LinkedIn.
- Hidden - View all contacts you've previously hidden from the main list.
- Remove Duplicates - See a list of contacts imported from different sources that you may want to merge into one contact.

To go back to the main list of categories after filtering by a category, click Filter by again and click to uncheck the category you were viewing.

Making New Connections

Growing your network on a continual basis is the best way to get the most out of LinkedIn as a prospecting tool. Every hand you shake, every phone call you make should be followed by a personalized LinkedIn request.

From the search bar at the top of your LinkedIn profile, type in the name of the person you're looking to connect with and choose them from the dropdown menu. If they don't appear, click the magnifying glass and choose from that list.

A last option would be to Google their name with the word LinkedIn and their public profile should appear.

1. Click into their profile
2. Click on the Connect button
3. Choose how you know them
4. Personalize the note below

Dear XXX,
It was a pleasure meeting you today at the Chamber of Commerce. I'd like to connect with you on LinkedIn and setup a brief call so we can explore ways that we might be able to work together.

Looking forward to speaking with you,

Brynne Tillman

When they accept your connection request:

Dear XXX,
It's nice to be connected here on LinkedIn. Let's set up a brief call to learn more about each other's respective businesses. I have Monday morning if there's an afternoon available for a conversation. Let me know what works best for you.

Looking forward to speaking with you,

Brynne Tillman

Back Door to Connections

If you want to send a message with your LinkedIn connection request, you often have to verify how you know this person, and it isn't very clear how to answer it all the time. In this example the best choice was "We've done business together" but I just met Bill at a networking meeting so is that accurate?

He is certainly not a colleague, or a classmate, and Friend is so awkward. Sadly We Share a Group option has gone away and if you choose other you need to add an email that I may not have.

Here are the directions to the back door!

1. Visit the profile of the person you are looking to connect with.

2. Click the star (relationship) button to save them as a connection.

3. Click on Connections on the top bar.

4. Choose Sort By Recent Conversations.

5. Click New.

6. Hover below their location and click connect.

7. Type your note and send. In this message, you can add your email or a link which is not available in a traditional connection request.

No need to answer "How do you know...".

BONUS: The LinkedIn App offers the option to send a personalized note. When on your prospective connections profile, click on the box with the arrow on the top right corner. You will be given the option to write a personal note...it is about time!

Building Rapport

Obviously, you should make preparations before you engage in any meeting, but you knew that! Then check out all the areas where you may have something in common. Do your due diligence; it will pay off big time!

Check out the full profile including all websites, twitter accounts, past employment and Alma Mater. Be sure to read their entire Summary and interests for some real insights into their business.

Here's an example of how this can help: Recently we met with a client that we expected to be a challenge. Scott was willing to meet with us, but hesitant to hire us. In prepping for our appointment, we looked through his LinkedIn profile before the appointment and noticed in passing that one of his interests was Boy Scouts.

As expected, there was initial resistance and building rapport was tough. As I looked around at the pictures in his office, I noticed his son reminding me of the Boy Scouts. "Scott", I said, "I noticed you were interested in the Boy Scouts. My twins are Cub Scouts and really love it."

For the next 10 minutes, that was all we talked about. All of the walls came down and the conversation began. While we secured the deal, we didn't get it because of our common interest. Scott became a client because we were a good fit. But without that ice-breaker we may never have connected.

The other important feature to look at is your shared connections. Look at who you and your prospect both know, make some calls, and then get some background.

When Nicole Bradley of ARAMARK was vetting LinkedIn training companies, we were among many that she was talking with. We knew that it was important to not only make a good impression, but to leverage our network to stand out. On LinkedIn we were both connected to Kim Richmond, a Professor, Marketer, Speaker and Author. Kim brings Brynne in to teach her students every semester. Brynne reached out to Kim and low and behold, Nicole was one of her former students and they had a fantastic relationship. Kim gave us 2 thumbs up and Nicole brought in Brynne. Ultimately, ARAMARK became our client (more on this story on page 36). Identifying mutual connections and reaching out for a recommendation can be just what we need to gain the competitive edge.

Five Techniques for Building Rapport

Rapport is the ability to relate to others in a way that creates a level of trust and understanding. Simply put, rapport is connection and it is important to build rapport with your prospects and clients as it gets them to be open to, accept and begin to process your suggestions.

Rapport is one of the most important features or characteristics of growing and sustaining relationships both personally and professionally.

In traditional sales they would teach matching your prospect's body, maintaining eye contact, and matching breathing rhythm, speech patterns and so forth. And, when meeting face-to-face these are all really important, but what happens when you begin building rapport online? The rules change.

Here are some important elements that can help build rapport with prospective buyers:

1. Research their background, hobbies, schools, and content they and their company are sharing on social media. To build rapport you don't have to like or agree with the content they share on social media, but you should read it and understand their position or thought process.

2. "Like", comment or share information that they have posted to social media. They are putting content out there for people to read and they are thrilled when you take the time to make what they shared matter.

3. Find and share articles and blogs that your prospect finds helpful; in fact, we have on occasion written a blog with a specific prospect in mind.

4. Respect the email boundaries; don't fill up your prospective client's inbox with too many back and forth messaging – take it offline. Set an appointment to meet or speak and begin to build rapport the old fashioned way!

5. Reach out to share connections to learn more about them personally and professionally.

What to Look for in a Profile

George Mach   1st
CEO | Helping Businesses Solve Technology Challenges | Business IT Outsourcing | Cloud Computing | IT Project Delivery
Greater Philadelphia Area | Information Technology and Services

Current   Apex IT Group
Previous Asellus Integration Technologies, Mach One Technologies, Inc.

Send a message

500+ connections

Background

 Summary

Seasoned Information Technology Executive. Deep industry knowledge around providing Managed IT Services Programs, IT Consulting Services and Cloud Computing Solutions to businesses of all size. I am Responsible for Corporate Leadership, Business Planning, Sales and Marketing, Accounting & Finance, Project Management Success, Process Development and Improvement, Forecasting and Financial Benchmarking.

IT High Value Solution Stack Experience with Microsoft, Cisco, Citrix, VM Ware, EMC, NetApp, Dell, HP, IBM, Barracuda Networks and other Industry Leading Technology Solutions.

Specialties: Mid Market IT Outsourcing, Healthcare IT, Non Profit Technology Consulting, Legal Indsutry Technology Solutions, Mechanical, Structural, Civil, Enviornmental Engineering Firm Technology Solutions.

> Read the summary, this is what they want you to know. It will give you insights into what is important to them.

 Honors & Awards

Philadelphia 100 Fastest Growing Companies
Wharton Small Business Development Center & The Philadelphia Business Journal
January 2012

Greater Philadelphia Area's Top 100 Fastest Growing Companies

Additional Honors & Awards

2010 South Jersey Top 25 Fastest Growing Companies #4 (fastest growing IT Services Company), Philadelphia Top 100 Fastest Growing Companies, Delaware Valley Young Entrepreneurs Award.

> Acknowledging awards such as honors that your prospect has received is a great way to connect.

Look at 'People Also Viewed' and 'People Similar to' on the right hand side of your connection's profile. These are often great prospects.

Experience

CEO
Apex IT Group
January 2007 – Present (7 years) | Pennsauken, New Jersey

Apex IT Group provides IT Solutions to companies in the Delaware Valley. Our core services include Strategic IT Consulting, IT Outsourcing Services, Cloud Services, & IT Project Services. We deliver results through our unique and proprietary proven process.

Our business is built to help our customers by taking the complexity out of IT with our simple yet effective "Zoom Out" approach to IT. We simplify the IT management process by first looking at the business: people, process and technologies. Through our unique process-driven IT Management Methodology, our people deliver consistent, predictable end results for our customers' businesses.

> Look at how he describes his responsibilities and recommendations.

Vice President of Sales & Marketing
Asellus Integration Technologies
February 2002 – 2006 (4 years) | Blackwood New Jersey

Responsible for All Sales Management, Inside Sales, Outside Sales, Proposal Development, Technical Sales Consulting, CRM Implementation, Account Management, Working with Sr. Network and Systems Engineers in Solution Design.

President
Mach One Technologies, Inc.
January 2000 – March 2003 (3 years 3 months)

Providing IT Consulting and Support Services

> Look at former places of employment as well as colleges.

> Be aware of the skills your prospect has listed on their profile to get an idea of how they identify themselves.

> Identify shared connections and reach out to them in advance of your meeting. This can be powerful in background research.

69

Your Groups

Finding the Right Groups

LinkedIn Groups are a fantastic way to create thought leadership, engage prospects and networking partners as well as brand yourself and your company as subject-matter experts. Through the right targeted groups and the appropriate discussions, you will quickly begin to attract prospects.

Groups are about engagement as well. Your participation in the group is critical. Read the news feeds and review the weekly updates that are emailed to you to see if there are discussions that are relevant to you.

When Nicole Bradley from ARAMARK was looking for training, she posted to a group and we responded. Others in the group, who knew what we do through our participation in discussions and posting relevant blogs, endorsed us. This gave Nicole the confidence to invest time in learning more and exploring if we were the right fit for ARAMARK. This sparked communication, and along with leveraging our shared connections, we were able to gain a meeting. ARAMARK is now our client. This is why it is critical to choose groups where your target prospects are members.

There are 3 easy ways to find the right groups:
1. Look at the groups your current clients are in because there is a good chance that they are industry groups where more people like them are hanging out.
2. In the search box at the top of any page, select Groups from the dropdown list on the left. Then type the keywords or titles of the people you wish to meet and search. On the search results page, you can drill down your search using the filters on the left.
3. Move your cursor over Interests at the top of your homepage and select Groups. Look for groups in the Groups you may be interested in the box at the bottom of the page.

Deciding if the group is right for you:

1. Click a group's name to view its Discussions page.
2. Click the Information and settings icon near the top right.
3. Click Group profile to see more information about the group and its members.

Posting to Groups

Just like posting to your homepage, you can start a discussion from your group's Discussions page.

1. Click Interest then Groups at the top of your home page.
2. Click the group's name that you are looking to post in.
3. Enter your topic or question in the "Start a discussion or share something with the group" box (required).
4. Enter details in the "Add more details" box (required).
5. Attach a link (optional).
6. Click Share.

This post will be in a group email to all the group members (unless they have personally opted-out in settings) along with all the other new and active discussions. It also goes into the new discussion feed and as other members comment and "like" your discussion, it will stay in the feed. The more activity there is around your discussion, the higher in the feed it will be.

Posting Blogs

If you can share your blog, you will begin to draw a lot of new visitors to your website. If you have Google analytics, you will be able to see the results. It should take less than a week to see the amount of traffic that your LinkedIn posts are generating.

If you are looking to get the most ROI from the visits to your blog, then you must have a few key elements:

1. The blog lives in your website, not as a separate entity. We want the visitors to explore the website and truly learn what it is we do and how we might be able to help them.
2. The headline or title of your blog needs to attract your target market. In fact, if you use the title of your prospect in the blog title, they are much more likely to click through it.
3. Have social "shares" on your blog. Make it easy for others to share your content.
4. Be sure that a call to action resides at the bottom of the blog: a whitepaper to download, a webinar to register for or simply 'join our email' for lead capture.

Posting a Poll

Polls are a great way to get engagement, gather great intel and begin meaningful business relationships. You can ask questions that your target market would like to answer verses questions around what you want to hear. Remember the key is to get engagement, to get on the radar of prospects and networking alliance partners, not to sell. Relationships evolve. They begin with knowing, then liking, and ultimately trusting. Business happens at the trusting stage, but believe me, it takes time to get there.

Polls are the get to know stage, and engaging conversation in comments becomes the like. Listening and caring about what others have to say, consistently offering engaging and educational content and converting the conversation offline is what will ultimately get them to trust you. This is a process and if you respect the process you will see success.

LinkedIn retired Polls in the Spring of 2014, but that won't stop us!

We recommend using an outside Poll site to create the question or questions you would like to ask, then use the link along with a discussion to get engagement. Why may it be better you ask? Because we can now post one poll and collect all the data in one place from every group or post. We can even share the link in an email or message and your contact doesn't have to share the group with you to vote!

Here is a short list of free sites:

1. Survey Monkey
2. Poll Code
3. Poll Maker
4. Easy Polls

You can actually message targeted group members individually here is how:

Dear XXX,

As a group member of XXX, I would like to introduce myself and share a link to a poll my company has posted. LINK HERE Your vote and participation would mean a lot to me. Also, please feel free to connect with my on LinkedIn as well!

YOUR NAME

Target Content

Just posting content into groups is valuable, but delivering your content directly to your target market is even better. Here is how you can use filters to identify the members of the group that you would like to engage.

1. In the group, click on the number of Members on the top right of the group menu.
2. In Search Members type in key words, titles and/ or location that you are using to filter. For example, if you are looking to identify just CEOs in a group, type CEO in the box. But, if you were looking to identify CEOs in NYC type "CEO" AND "New York City". This is known as a Boolean search. You can use AND, NOT, OR but be sure to capitalize them for LinkedIn searches.
3. A list of members will appear. From this menu you are able to invite them to connect or send them a message, even if you are not connected!
4. Click Send message.
5. Write a message:

Hello XXX,
We just posted a blog that we thought might be helpful for Sales Directors. I would appreciate your feedback. www.BLOGURLHERE.com

OR

Hello XXX,
We just posted a poll and as a Sales Director, your vote and feedback would mean a lot to us.
www.POLLURL.com

This is an activity that you can have an intern or administrative assistant (or us!) handle.

Be sure you are sharing content that your prospects want to read, not information you want to share. Everyone listens to the infamous radio station WIIFM – What's In It For Me?

When we read an article or watch a video we are spending our precious time. Make sure your viewers walk away from your content feeling that it was time well-spent. Typically we like to leave a key take-away, something our readers can implement right away or something that gets them thinking beyond the article. This is the foundation of becoming a true thought leader.

"Boolean" AND "Search"

The search feature allows you to search LinkedIn multiple ways (including Boolean searches). You can specify what type of search you would like to run by selecting from the search menu one of the drop down menus mentioned below. In some cases an "Advanced" link is made available to the right of the "Search" button.

Quoted searches: If you would like to search for an exact phrase, you can enclose the phrase in quotation marks. Example: If you want to find Profiles that contain the words "product manager", in that exact order, type the following in for your search: "product manager."

Advanced Search lets us know very quickly who in our warm market knows who we want to meet. The prospecting power when leveraging this tool is endless. Spend a little time and get to know Advanced Searches. They will be your new best friend!

AND searches: If you would like to search for Profiles which include two terms, you can separate those terms with the upper-case word AND. However, you don't have to use AND; if you enter two terms, it will assume that order concept. Example: Find profiles that have all the words "Sales" AND "Manager" AND "Philadelphia" – the search will get results that include profiles that have all three.

OR searches: If you would like to search for Profiles which include just one of two or more terms, you can separate those terms with the upper-case word OR. Example: If you want to find Profiles containing either CEO or President, type the following in for your search: "CEO" OR "President" and your results will give you all the CEOs and all the Presidents.

NOT searches: If you would like to do a search but exclude a particular term, type that term with a NOT immediately before it. Example: If you want to get a list of CEOs, but avoid seeing any Profile containing the word "computer", type the following in for your search: "CEO" NOT "computer" and your results will give you all the CEOs that do not have the word computer in the profile.

Create a Group

Managing a group can be very powerful, but it does take a lot of nurturing, refereeing and encouraging engagement and discussion. One real benefit of your own group is the ability to send a weekly group announcement that goes into every group members email inbox. Before you start a group, it is critical that you determine why you want a group, what your goal of the group is and what the rules of engagement are. For example, we started The Linked User Group, completely for the purpose of sharing LinkedIn ideas and strategies and as a forum for professionals to ask questions and get relevant answers from experts around the globe.

To create a group (of which you will be the owner) take the following steps:

1. Click on Groups Tab.
2. Click Create a Group.
3. Choose a logo (you can create your own in PowerPoint, screenshot it, edit in Paint and save it as a JPEG 100KB in size).
4. Name your group and choose Group type that is relevant to your mission.
5. Write a summary about your group's purpose and a description as it appears.
6. Add a relevant website or a blog that it relates to (not mandatory).
7. Add Group Owner Email and Access (Auto-join or Request to join).
8. Add pre-approved members, location, and Twitter, check to agreement and choose open or members-only group Save.

Benefit	Open Group	Members Only
Discussion Visibility	Anyone	Members Only
Indexing by search engines	Yes	No
Sharing on Twitter & Facebook	Yes	No
Anyone can post	Manager Option	No

Group Templates

It is important to set up your templates so that you have messaging to the folks looking to join your group at each stage:

1. Click on Manage.
2. Click Templates on the bottom right.
3. Write what they will see when they Request to Join and when they have been accepted. You can also write a decline message for closed groups and a decline and block message for people who are spamming the group.

Share Your Group

Once you have your group, you will want people to join it. Make sure you are matching your invitees to the mission and purpose of the group.

1. Click on Manage.
2. Click on Send invitation.
3. Add up to 50 of your first connections.
4. Customize note and Send. Be sure to uncheck "Allow Recipients" to hide each other's names and email addresses.

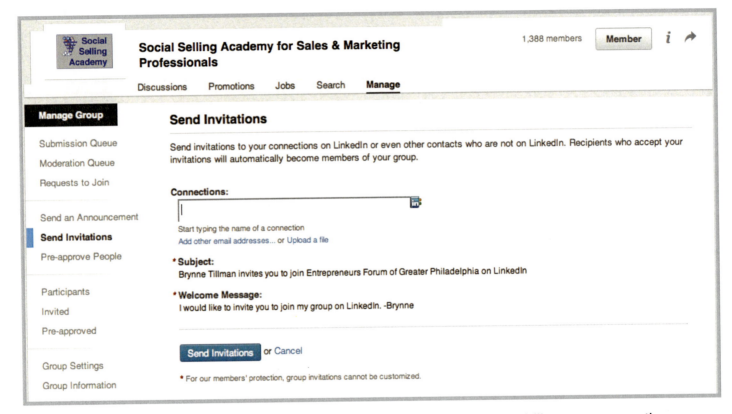

You have access to all of your group members and the ability to message them individually.

1. Click on Manage.
2. Click on Participants.
3. Click on Members tab.
4. Filter by last name or date joined group.
5. Click message button below their name and send private messages.

You can export your connections into an excel spreadsheet, as we discussed before, and import the list through upload file. This allows you to invite all your connections at one time. You can actually invite up to 18,000 people to your group through uploading emails.

Engage Members

A group is only as good as its activity. Ask your members to share their thoughts on hot topics. Ask them to post questions or share insights and be sure to comment and re-share their content. Check out what some of your members are posting on their personal updates and reach out to ask that they share the same material in the group.

If someone posts good quality content, as the group manager you can add it to Manager's Choice and it remains on the top right of the group, for all to see. It will also be showcased in the group update emails.

One of the great benefits to having your own group is that you are able to send out an announcement that goes into every member's inbox. Make sure this information is of benefit to them and not soliciting their own business. This is a great way to keep in front of your members and keep them engaged on a weekly basis.

It is up to you to keep it going, keep it relevant and keep it effective. This is no small task, so know what you are getting yourself into!

Grow your group by inviting industry thought leaders, popular bloggers and influential tweeters to share their content in your group. A fabulous automated tool for identifying influential bloggers and reaching out to them through customized templates is Pitchbox.com.

Dear XXX,

I have been following your content for some time, and I really enjoyed your latest blog "XXX". I would be honored if you would be willing to share one of your blogs in my LinkedIn Group NAME AND URL. I believe my group members would benefit from your content, and you would gain a few more followers for sure. Thank you in advance for your consideration.

Your Network

Make Connections

We are not saying that our strategy here is "give to get". It's more like paying it forward. If we can help others succeed it will come back to us many fold. Becoming a business connector is one of the most prevailing ways to create a reputation and attract others to you.

Traditionally, we would call these folks "Centers of Influence" – professionals we all would like to take to coffee, pick their brain, and learn how they got to where they are now. They are successful and have made a difference in others' lives – as that is what makes them powerful influencers in the business world.

"How can I establish a reputation as a business connector?" you ask.

1. Detach from what you will get out of it.
2. Invest the time in learning about others and who they want to meet.
3. Take notes on each person in your network.
4. Ask your folks for a paragraph on how they would like to be introduced.
5. Make it a practice to make at least 1 meaningful introduction to everyone you meet.
6. Go through your network and make proactive introductions on a consistent basis.
7. Offer your new contacts to go through your connections and identify a few people that they would like to meet.
8. Do not stop your other networking. This doesn't take place of the face-to-face interaction, it just makes it more efficient.
9. Be a good source of industry or market insights that are relevant to your network.

Be sure to connect with everyone you meet. Networkers, Co-Workers, Clients, even people you meet in the grocery line.

XXX,

It was a pleasure to meet you today at XXX. Let's connect on LinkedIn and explore ways that we might be able to work together. In addition, please let me know the types of people you are looking to meet so I can make some introductions on your behalf.

Networking Relationships

Most professionals that are responsible for business development have a professional network. There are 4 types of relationships that work well with our LinkedIn strategy:

1. Weekly or monthly groups that have one professional per industry and the intent is to make introductions to one another.
2. Informal networking relationships that were made at business card exchanges, associations or professional events that are worthy of meeting 1:1 for exploration on how you may be able to help each other out.
3. Centers of Influence are those with strong relationships that are well connected to the business community that know, trust and like you but are not related to your industry.
4. Strategic Alliances, such as vendors and other sales professionals that work with like decision-makers and are not competitors.

Networking to Prospecting

A good way to break into a company is to network with their sales people. It is very simple to call a company and ask to speak with their top sales person, there are no gatekeepers here! It is important to ask for a top performer because you will be making introductions on their behalf, and you want to know that they are good at what they do. Here is what you might say:

Hello XXX,

I am looking forward to meeting you for coffee on Thursday and exploring further how we may be able to help each other out. Once we have connected on LinkedIn, please feel free to look through my connections and write down the people you would like to meet and we can review your selections together.

Build your network and expand your reach.

1. Consider starting a monthly referral source group.
2. Run Speed Networking or Round Table Networking events.
3. Join Associations, Board of Directors and Committees.
4. Become an ambassador of a Chamber of Commerce or similar groups.
5. At events, ask each professional you meet who they would like to meet. When you meet those folks throughout the night, proactively make the introductions for them.
6. Carry a list of the prospects or referral partners that you'd like to make introductions to.

This is just the beginning, but if you are consistent and authentic in your approach – it will work. And, when they come up on that 2nd generation search and you request a warm introduction, they will be more than happy to make that happen.

Warm Network

With over 350 million members, growing a network has endless opportunities. And, of course, building a new network filled with professionals that we didn't know we didn't know is very cool. But what about the people in our network that we have known for years, the ones we see at business card exchanges, meet for coffee or lunch periodically or even sit on a board with…what about them?

Fostering your current network can be as or even more important than growing a new one. Who is your hottest market? We have our families and flat tire friends (anyone you can call in the middle of the night when you have a flat tire to come pick you up). Then there are your Saturday night double date friends, your going to the movies friends and colleagues from work. And, if you are a good networker you have your professional groups and strategic alliances.

Be thoughtful about this next assignment. Make a list of the top 5 people in your life who you could ask for introductions knowing that they would give them to you with few questions asked. That is where we will begin with our warm market.

Name	Relationship	Industry	3 People They Are Connected To On LinkedIn

Give First

Networking is a two way street. As you're building relationships and referral sources it is vital that you make meaningful introductions to your network connections. Be sure to identify exactly the types of prospects and strategic alliances that your networking partners are looking to meet and then record the attributes in the notes section in their profile. After each meeting, look through your connections and proactively make introductions that would be beneficial to both parties.

Make Introductions

Hello Friend 1 and Friend 2,

I hope this note finds you well. I am using LinkedIn to expand my network as well as connect other professionals with each other. The purpose of my email today is to make this introduction, as I believe there could be some synergy between the two of you.

Friend 1 does lots of great things with widgets.
friend.1@email.com
www.friend1company.com
(215) 555.1212

Friend 2 does lots of great things with widgets.
friend.2@email.com
www.friend2company.com
(215) 555.1212

Enjoy networking! If either of you would like introductions to specific people that I am connected to, please let me know. I would be happy to make those introductions as well.

If your contact says just reach out and use my name:

Copy your contact (Joe) and the new person (Frank) in an email:
Joe, thank you for the connection.

Frank,
I had noticed you were connected to Joe on LinkedIn and he mentioned I should reach out to you directly. I am the CEO of Social Sales Link, a social selling training company. I would like to set up a phone call and explore ways we might work together. I have Monday morning and Thursday afternoon open, do either work for you?

LinkedIn & Coffee Meetings

Networking is critical for B2B sales people, but often it isn't nearly as productive as we would like or need it to be. We invest our time in networking events such as chamber meetings, meetups, business card exchanges etc., but often it doesn't convert to sales.

Yes, I said it...sales. I know, I used that taboo word when it comes to networking, but think about it, did you leave your family at home on a Tuesday night so you could meet your new BFF? Of course not, and neither did the other 42 people in the room. You are all there to get business. The key is, don't attend the event looking for your next prospect, go with the mindset that you are there to meet people that you can mutually refer business to one another. Often the follow-up is coffee. So, let's make that meeting productive! If you aren't connected on LinkedIn with your new networking partner, that is your first step, then send this note:

XXX, I am looking forward to our coffee meeting next week. Please feel free to look through my LinkedIn connections and make a list of people that you might want to meet. I will do the same and we can review the list when we are together.

1. From their profile, **click on their blue connections** number (500+)
2. This takes you to their connections where you will see a search bar in the top right (**click on the magnifying glass**)
3. Enter the **keywords or title** of the people you would like to meet ie. "CIO" OR "CTO" OR "IT Director" **Enter** and then Click **advanced** in the top left of the box
4. Use the left hand side filters to **drill down** like location and/or industry
5. **Make a list** of who your networking partner knows that you would like to meet and Review their names when you are together and whittle them down to a select few that are the best fit
6. **Exchange introduction** templates ie.
   I would like to introduce you to Brynne Tillman, CEO of Social Sales Link. I thought it might make sense for the two of you to connect and investigate how you might work together. Brynne helps sales professionals build their pipeline, reduce the sales cycle and close more business through leveraging the power of LinkedIn and Social Selling. Brynne will be contacting you in the next couple of days, please take her call; I believe it will be well worth your time. If you would like to reach out sooner, her contact information is: Brynne.Tillman@SocialSalesLink.com | 888.775.5262 http://www.linkedin.com/in/brynnetillman
7. Copy your networking partner and each person you are introducing in a LinkedIn message or email with their paragraph, and have them do the same.
8. **Reply All**: Networking Partner, thank you for the introduction. New Person, I am looking forward to speaking with you, learn more about you and your business and explore ways we might be able to work together. I have Monday morning and Thursday afternoon available for a call, what works best for you?

Closed Contacts

If you find that your connection is only showing your shared connections – it is because they chose to keep their network private.

Try this:

Dear XXX,

I am looking forward to our meeting on XXX and exploring further how we can help each other. Attached is a copy of my LinkedIn connections. Please feel free to look through them and highlight anyone you would like an introduction to. We can review your selections together during our meeting. If you would be open to doing the same, below are the step-by-step instructions on how to export your connections.

Thank you!
Brynne Tillman

Directions to export connections into an Excel spreadsheet and share it:

1. Hover over Network and select Contacts from the dropdown.
2. Click the Settings Gear on the top right corner.
3. Click the Export Connections link in the bottom right corner of the page.
4. Enter the security text when prompted.
5. Click Export.
6. Save the file in a location where you can easily find it, like your computer's desktop.

Note: If you're using Internet Explorer and see a yellow pop-up blocker across the top of the page, click the yellow bar and then select Download File.

6. Open the spreadsheet and clean it up by deleting all columns except FIRST NAME, LAST NAME, JOB TITLE and COMPANY NAME. Do not share the email address of your connections.

7. Save the file in a location where you can easily find it, like your desktop. Attach it to an email and send.

Advanced Search

There are many ways to leverage advanced searches, and we urge you to spend some time exploring them. This is the quintessential "working smarter not harder." Advanced Search quickly lets you know who in your warm market knows whom you want to meet. The prospecting power when leveraging this tool is endless. Spend a little time and get to know Advanced Searches – it will be your new best friend!

1. Click on the Advanced Search hyperlink next to the magnify glass on the top right the dropdown.
2. Choose keywords that represent your target market.
3. And/or Title (you can choose from the drop down current, past or both – in addition, you can use Boolean searches here.
4. Fill out geographic preferences and industry choices.
5. Choose relationships (1st, 2nd, 3rd, Group).
6. Search and you will get a list of exactly who you are looking for.

The magic lives in the 2nd degree connections, so be sure to click 2nd in Relationship. This will give us a list of who knows who we want to know - and we can ask for introductions!

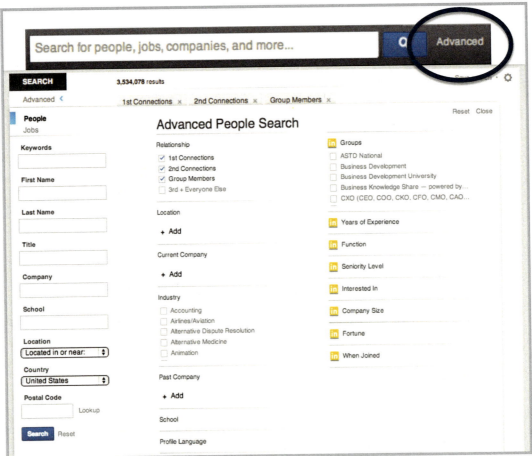

88

LinkedIn & Social Selling For Business Development

The Save

Once you have your perfect search you can save it for later. Just click Save Search on the top right hand side of the search, name it, and click the green checkmark to save it for later. You can save 3 searches using the free LinkedIn account.

Not only can you retrieve these searches on demand, but on a weekly basis LinkedIn will update the new folks entering your network who fall under the search criteria. When we help our clients come up with a LinkedIn prospecting plan, this is the number one activity that they are encouraged to do every week. Think about this: you have created your ideal criteria (hopefully leveraging the 2nd generation search) one time, and LinkedIn is kind enough to keep you in the loop when new professionals who meet those criteria join your network. So, last week we connected with 5 new contacts – and didn't have the time to look through their connections to see who they know that I may want an introduction to.

But luckily, we have a saved search: VPs of Sales within 50 miles of my zip code that are a 2nd connection. Every Monday morning we log into LinkedIn, click on saved searches and see that we have 10 new professionals within our network that meet those criteria. We then click the hyperlink "view" and the full list comes up in the window. We can then click on shared connection and ask for our warm introduction. POWERFUL stuff, do you agree?

There is no easier, more productive way to identify new prospects as they enter your network, whether through a new connection of yours, or one of your current contacts' new connections.

Saved Searches

Type	Title	New	Alert	Created
People	Sales Managers 2nd	20	Weekly	Sep 22, 2013
People	Sales Trainers 2nd	43	Weekly	Sep 22, 2013
People	President, CEO 25 mi (40 km)	173	Monthly	Dec 13, 2010

The Update

Based on your email alert status (weekly or monthly) you will receive an email to your primary account with a list of the new people in your network that meet your saved search criteria. To find your search proactively click on "Advanced", click on the gear on the top right and click "saved searches".

Leverage Public Profiles

Everyone has a public profile on LinkedIn. In fact, earlier we customized our URL so we could add it to our business cards and signature. When using a free account and logged into LinkedIn, the funny thing is that you are limited to the information you can see when you find a 3rd connection or beyond. Well, we thought, there is a public profile living out there. Let's go find it.

1. Copy the context headline.
2. Paste it into Google.
3. Type in the word LinkedIn and 'Enter'

If the LinkedIn profile doesn't come up from the headline search, use a Boolean search and put it in quotes "Chief Marketing Officer" AND "Neil M. B." It isn't 100%, but it has worked many times.

If you find yourself doing this search a lot, you might consider upgrading your LinkedIn account, as you will be able to see the full names of all the LinkedIn members.

The Company Search

If you ever cold call again without searching a company on LinkedIn to identify who is already in your network, you are certainly missing the boat, spinning your wheels, working harder not smarter… the idioms could go on and on.

Before we ever make the first call to a new prospect we have no known connection with (a typical cold call), we search the Company on LinkedIn to find out who in our network can provide an introduction for us.

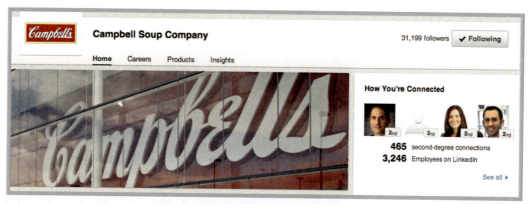

Example: In this case, if we're prospecting Campbell Soup, we pull up their profile to see if there is anyone at the company who we know. Initially we see that we have no 1st connections, we don't know anyone directly that works at Campbell Soup, however we learn that there are 465 2nd generation connections that we can reach out and ask for a warm introduction. We click the 465 and the list comes up for our perusing.

We find someone on our list that is closest to the title of our ideal prospect, or is at least in the department. Any warm connection, regardless of their position, is more powerful than any cold call can ever be. Again, we click on Shared Connection(s) and ask for our warm introduction. Easy, right?

 You can filter your selections on the right hand side and scroll down. And, once again, you can identify who you know that knows the person you want to speak with at that company. There is enormous power in this feature – use it!

91

The Client

Customer service and delivery is the most important part of a client relationship. Once you have ensured that your deliverables are meeting their expectations, the door is open to ask for more.

As sales trainers and coaches, we believe client marketing is one of the best ways to grow your business. There are 5 key components that you should be focused on:

1. Maintaining the current business.
2. Get internal introductions and additional business.
3. External Introductions and referrals.
4. Testimonials and recommendations.
5. Vendors.

Getting more business may be as simple as asking, but are you asking for other internal introductions to other people within the organization that may need your products and services? There are 2 ways to identify who you want to meet within the company:

1. Check out your client's Company Profile and identify who else in the company you would like to meet. Click on your first or second-degree connections or see all and you can make your list of the folks you'd like to meet. When you are with your client, you can ask them for an introduction.

2. You can also go to Advanced Search, type in the company and title of the person or people that you would like to meet, click Search and write down the names you would like to review with your client. Simple.

LinkedIn & Social Selling For Business Development

Referrals

External Introductions and referrals are key to growing business. A good business development professional asks for introductions, and typically the conversation goes something like this:

Salesperson: "Ms. Client, thank you very much for your business. Are you happy with the products and services we have been able to help you with over the last few months?"
Client: "Oh, yes, Mr. Salesperson. We have been very happy and we love working with you and your company."
Salesperson: "That is terrific, Ms. Client. The way we grow our business has always been through introductions and recommendations from our satisfied clients. By any chance, do you know of anyone else that could use our products and services?"
Client: "Hmm, let me see. I can't think of anyone off hand right now, but if I do think of someone I will certainly be happy to introduce you."

Bummer – not exactly how we had hoped it would go. But now we have LinkedIn as a powerful tool and this conversation will be much more productive. Before you go out on the client visit, do the following:

1. Connect with your client on LinkedIn.
2. Suggest they look through your connections as you would be happy to make introductions on their behalf.
3. Check out their contacts from the search bar as we discussed in the networking section.
4. Make a list of 5 prospects that meet your criteria and bring the list with you.

And here is how the conversation may go now:

Client: "Hmm, let me see. I can't think of anyone off hand right now, but if I think of someone I will certainly be happy to introduce you."
Salesperson: "Ms. Client, when we connected on LinkedIn I noticed that you were linked to a few folks who would be great introductions for me. Would it be alright if I ran them by you?"
Client: "Of course, I would be happy to help!" (You may end up with 2 out of the 5 that they are willing to introduce you to for one reason or another.)
Salesperson: "Thank you so much for offering to make these introductions. You can just copy us both in an email and I can take it from there. To make it easier for you, would you like me to send you a short introduction paragraph that you can use?"
Client: "That would be great, thanks."
Salesperson: "I will get that to you by the end of the day. Also, I would be happy to make introductions for you as well. Who are you looking to meet?"

If we did just this for each of our clients, our pipeline could easily double and the business would follow!

Request Recommendations

Testimonials and recommendations can be best captured when your client mentions how happy they are with you and your company. Maybe it is just a moment of gratitude or a positive story of how you have impacted their business. Simply use the steps and verbiage from the profile section of this workbook.

Use these testimonials in your sales process with your prospects. You can start following your first meeting. Connect with your prospect on LinkedIn and say:

"Ms. Prospect, thank you for your time today. I am looking forward to our next meeting on Thursday. Let's connect on LinkedIn. Please feel free to look through some of the recommendations our clients have made on both my personal page and our company page."

This not only helps add credibility, but can help you close business faster. It may be enough that you won't have to give them references, which can add weeks to your sales cycle.

Lex Daniele, Assistant Vice President of Strategic Marketing at Affinity Insurance Services, a division of Aon Corporation
Greater Philadelphia Area

Leveraging LinkedIn for Business Development was one of the best educational opportunities I've attended in years. I highly recommend this class to anyone who is looking for ways to help increase their business development skills and business in general. Great for sales producers, marketers....everyone! Eye-opening for sure!

February 8, 2012 · Comment · Flag · Delete

Vendor Relationships

Client vendors, as we mentioned in the Center of Influence (COI) section of the workbook, are professionals that sell to the same decision maker we sell but are not our competitors. They are one of the best strategic networking sources we may have. Here is how we may ask our clients to share their other vendors with us:

"Mr. Client, I am currently growing my database with good vendors so if my clients ever need a referral, then I can pull the best of the best network. May I ask you, who are your currently using for website and marketing?" "Do you like them? If their answer is "Yes", ask "Would you mind if I contact them and drop your name?" If no, offer to introduce them to the good ones you now have relationships with.

This is a win/win for sure.

What to say to the vendor when you call:

"Hi, I am XXX. We both work with ABC company and I thought it might make sense for us to have a conversation. We are really looking to grow our business this year, and as we are both working with like industries, there may be an opportunity to help each other out. Would you be open to meeting for coffee next week and exploring ways in which we may be able to refer business to each other?"

LinkedIn & Social Selling For Business Development

The Introduction Templates

Dear Friend,

I hope this note finds you well. As you may know, I am leveraging LinkedIn to grow my network and noticed that you are connected to XXX at XXX. I was wondering if you would kindly provide an introduction for me. If you could copy us both in an email or LinkedIn message I can take it from there. To make it easier for you, I have included a short paragraph below that you are welcome to copy and paste.

Also, please feel free to look through my connections, I am happy to make introductions for you as well.

Thanks so much!
Brynne

GENERIC:

I would like to introduce you to Brynne, CEO of Social Sales Link. I thought it might make sense for the two of you to connect and investigate how you might work together. Brynne helps sales professionals build their pipeline, reduce the sales cycle and close more business through leveraging the power of LinkedIn and social selling. Brynne's LinkedIn programs have made a significant impact on the way her professionals are growing their business. Brynne will be contacting you in the next couple of days, please take her call; I believe it will be well worth your time. If you would like to reach out to Brynne, her contact information is:

Brynne.Tillman@socialsaleslink.com | 888.775.5262
http://www.linkedin.com/in/brynnetillman

CLIENT: (each one must be semi-customized)
I would like to introduce you to Brynne, CEO of Social Sales Link. We have worked with Brynne for the last year, and she has helped our sales team increase their qualified appointments and close more business. Through her classes and coaching, we have well exceeded our goals this year. I thought it might make sense for the two of you to talk and explore if Brynne might be able to help you and your team out as well. Brynne will be calling you in the next few days, please take her call, I think it will be well worth your time.
If you would like to reach out to Brynne, her contact information is:

Brynne.Tillman@socialsaleslink.com | 888.775.5262
http://www.linkedin.com/in/brynnetillman

Reply to Intro

Reply All to the email:

Friend, thank you so much for the introduction.

New Friend,

I am looking forward to meeting you and exploring ways that we might be able to work together. I have time Monday morning and Thursday afternoon for a call. Please let me know if either of those work.

Write Your Intro Template

Stranger Request

New Connection Request from Someone You Don't Know

This is always an interesting dilemma. Our suggestion is to evaluate if this is someone that would bring value to your network whether as a prospect, referral sources or as an introduction for one of your existing contacts. If the answer is yes, then we want to reply but not accept yet. Click on the arrow next to the accept button and respond to the invitation as follows.

Hi XXX,

Thank you for your LinkedIn connection invitation. I typically like to get to know the professionals I am connecting with to understand how they are using LinkedIn and see if we can help each other out in the networking world. At your convenience, I would like to set up a phone conversation, I can be reached at 888.775.5262.

I am looking forward to talking with you.

Brynne.Tillman@socialsaleslink.com | 888.775.5262
http://www.linkedin.com/in/brynnetillman

All of this messaging is for template purposes. In many situations it makes sense to just pick up the phone and have a conversation. The templates can help guide those conversations because the power in the dialogue far outweighs any email you can send.

If you find that you are retyping or copy and pasting templates a lot, check out TextExpander for Mac or Text Expander for Windows. This is the best investment we have ever made! Create entire emails and messages and a short code. Any time you want to use the template, type the short code and the entire message will appear. This isn't limited to LinkedIn either, it works everywhere on your computer.

Competitor's Request to Connect

Depending on your industry, you may believe there is more harm than good when it comes time to connecting with your competitors. If this is your belief you can respond to a connection request with:

Dear XXX,
Thank your request to connect with me on LinkedIn. I am going to have to respectfully decline, as connecting with my competition creates temptation for me! I wish you a prosperous year!

Research & Insights

Insights Selling

Insights Selling is made of two distinct moving parts. The first is about listening and learning as much as you can about your prospect prior to your first meeting. This can make the difference in first impressions, credibility and ultimately your positioning when the vendor decision is made. The second is understanding what is important to them and offering quality information and insights that are not just meaningful, but not available anywhere else. This is expressed through a combination of experience and research. If you are selling too many different industries, this could be an ongoing project, but over time you will build a library of valuable intel that can be used and reused – just tweaked appropriately for each new opportunity.

This process isn't a quick exercise, but it is critical, especially for winning a larger more complex sale. Moreover, this can be adapted to most businesses either by simplifying the steps or customizing them specific to your sales process.

Thought leadership, as we discussed earlier in the book, can be a game changer when used in prospecting appointments. Most insights will come to you after the research has been completed, but many of your foundational insights will carry over from client to client. It is your job to take your value proposition, your solutions and what you bring to the table and adapt it to each client's situation. This isn't about giving away your secret sauce or offering all of your solutions for free, but is about sharing some of your ideas that they can relate to and even implement and see results. When they see the value that you bring, and they are ready to select a vendor, you will have established a competitive edge.

Research is certainly not limited to LinkedIn. We encourage you to investigate company websites, press releases, annual reports, organizational charts and other public information. LinkedIn is just a piece, albeit a powerful one. There are 5 buckets to fill with background research:

1. The Company
2. The Decision Makers
3. The Industry
4. The Competition
5. Their Clients

If you equip yourself with background you will be able to match up your insights and position yourself with your prospects as the vendor that understands them and can make a positive impact.

The following pages can act as a guide when it comes to your research, but don't limit yourself to this section. It is important that you adapt this methodology to work for you and your company's selling process.

Use the advanced search feature to identify past employees, particularly ones that have worked in your targeted department. Identify how you are connected to or have a shared connection and request a conversation. Past employees are more likely to share what is happening inside a company than current employees. You can get intel through these connections that you may not be able to get anywhere else. If you share a group with them, you can copy their name, put it in the search bar in the members tab of the group and message the profile directly from there. That's just another great LinkedIn feature!

Company Research

Doing research on a company, particularly a mid-sized company or larger is relatively easy, just be prepared to invest some time. Look for what they want you to know (all the things they post) and all the things that are being said about them. Here are some of the things to look for:

LinkedIn Page
1. Staff – this can help you understand the organization and uncover some names and titles that could be part of the decision making process, and connect with them.
2. Updates show what they care about
3. Products and services tab and read about all of the prospects offerings
4. Featured Groups – these are groups that the company promotes and are part of – so consider joining the group and reading the feed, feature posts and purpose.
5. People also viewed (this is a list of other company pages, often this is their competitors and will give you other companies to do some background research on as well. This overlaps into the industry research)

Website
1. Locations.
2. News.
3. Blogs.
4. About Us.
5. Press Releases.
6. Products and Services.

Google
1. Press Releases.
2. Articles.
3. Awards.

Twitter & Facebook Pages
1. Followers.
2. Following.
3. Postings.
4. Retweets.

5. Annual Report(s)

6. Stock Fluctuations/Prices

 Be sure to check out 'People Also Viewed' to help you develop new prospect opportunities.

Decision Makers

Getting the background on the decision maker(s) is a critical element when gathering information on a company. The first step is to identify who your typical contacts are within your clients. Make a list of all the titles and departments that have been part of your sales process and match that with the organizational chart of your prospect. Build out an organizational chart for each prospect and fill it in through LinkedIn intel, website bios, phone calls and conversations. Understand what each of the decision makers care about and how your solution helps them and affects them. Be clear on what part of your solution will best serve each decision maker and be able to articulate it clearly.

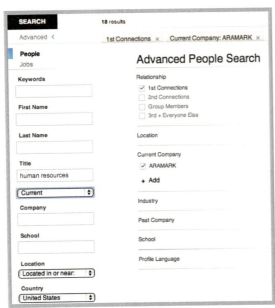

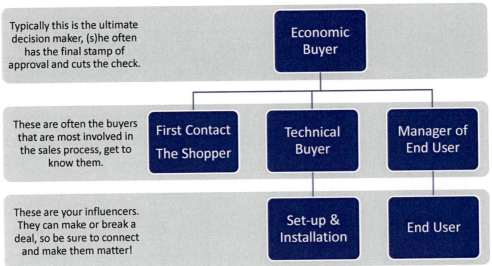

- **Economic Buyer** — Typically this is the ultimate decision maker, (s)he often has the final stamp of approval and cuts the check.
- **First Contact / The Shopper**, **Technical Buyer**, **Manager of End User** — These are often the buyers that are most involved in the sales process, get to know them.
- **Set-up & Installation**, **End User** — These are your influencers. They can make or break a deal, so be sure to connect and make them matter!

Review the rapport building section in this book, it will apply beautifully here. And don't forget to use the power of your own network.

Industry

Learning about a new prospect's industry should begin with a bank of targeted questions that lead you to relevant answers that relate to the solution(s) your product(s) or service(s) provide. Here are some questions that you may seek out the answers for in your research:

1. What are the products and services your client sells?
2. Who do they sell to?
    1. Do their clients need or want what they sell?
    2. Are there many other options other than their products or services?
3. News, Trends and Forecasts
    1. Where is the industry now?
    2. Where might it be in 6 months, 1 year, 3 years?
    3. Is the industry stagnate or scaling up or down?
4. Economic Indicators
    1. What factors might influence how the industry is doing?
    2. Is the industry cyclical or non-cyclical?
5. Market Share
    1. Who are the dominant players and/or the direct competition in the industry?
    2. Is the market for the company local, regional, national or international?
6. Innovation
    1. Does the industry rely on new products or services?
    2. Does it grow through new offerings?
    3. Does your prospect need to continually innovate to stay relevant in the market?
7. Legal and Regulatory Issues
    1. What are the current or future regulatory issues which might affect the industry?
    2. What are the major state, federal or international bodies which might have influence?
    3. Are the any possible pending bills or regulations which might have significant impact?
8. Where are Industry Updates?
    1. Trade Publications
    2. Industry Associations or Organizations
    3. Trade Shows & Conventions
    4. Governmental Information
    5. Press Releases & Articles
    6. Twitter
    7. LinkedIn Groups - join groups that your prospects are in, especially industry related ones - you will get a lot of insight into their current market and industry conditions.

If you really want to understand the company you are prospecting, don't just research their industry, but also research the industry they sell into. If you understand their client you are closer to understanding them.

Social Selling

What is Social Selling?

There is a significant shift in the way that people are buying, which means we have to shift the way we are selling. The Internet changed everything. It used to be the only way a client could find out how we could help them was to engage us. Now, they Google. Prospects identify all the competition, research and come up with pros and cons lists and begin to form an opinion. An opinion either you can shape or your competition can. Studies have proven over and over again that 60-70% of buying decisions are made before a sales person is even involved in the conversation.

We must do four things to get an edge:

1. Listen: Research to identify what your prospect cares about and needs. By discovering what articles they like, what blogs they share, who they are connected to and other social media activities, we can begin to understand our prospects in ways we never could before.

2. Educate: Branding you and your company as the subject matter expert. Then create and share educational content that engages a specific community through social platforms and converts to leads.

3. Prospect: Leverage social media for networking and client warm referrals and introductions.

4. Position: Research and gather intelligence to be leveraged in rapport building, proposed client solutions, defining statement of work and ultimately setting the bar that influences the sale.

Why Social Selling?

Sales Professionals need to position themselves as the thought leader and industry expert. They need to be the ones influencing their prospects buying decisions and participating in their choice even before they are engaged.

Then, we need to listen. Collect enough intel about the company, the industry, the market conditions and the culture before we ever show up. We need to identify who the decision makers are, what is important to them and what they actually need in order to position the right solution.

If the Sales Professional shows up and conducts another typical sales call with "tell me about your pain" they will lose. They need to come into the game knowing their pain in advance, educating them through strategies and stories on how others have fixed the pain and talk about their dreams. People run from pain, but gravitate toward pleasure. If you believe in The Secret, that the energy you put out is the energy you attract, then put out success, not pain. Put out achievement not loss.

Before we get into the meat of Social Selling, we need to begin with basic knowledge so the next few pages are an overview of the key elements that go into a successful social selling program.

Twitter Talk

Twitter is an online social networking and microblogging service that enables users to send and read "tweets", which are text messages limited to 140 characters. Users can read and post tweets. Users access Twitter through the website or mobile device applications. It is a very powerful newsfeed that has not only made a significant impact on business but on the world. Instantly, millions of people can get real time news. Before we get into strategy, here is a brief decoding to make you comfortable with the twitter lingo.

- A user's **"Twitter handle"** is the username they have selected and the accompanying URL, like so: http://twitter.com/username.

- A **Tweet** is a message posted via Twitter containing 140 characters or fewer.

- The # symbol is used to identify keywords or topics in a Tweet. It can be used next to any word that is important to the content in the tweet. We recommend never having more than 3 # in any tweet, it waters down its importance.

- The @ sign is used to mention a user in a tweet, like this: Hello @Twitter! When a username is preceded by the @ sign, it becomes a link to that Twitter profile.

- An **Avatar** is an image that you have uploaded to represent your Twitter profile.

- Click on the Connect tab to view who has **favorited** or **retweeted** your Tweets, who has recently followed you, and all of your **@replies** and **@mentions**.

- **Direct Message** is also called a DM, these Tweets are private between the sender and recipient. Tweets become DMs when they begin with "**d username**" to specify whom the message is for.

- To favorite a Tweet **click the yellow star** next to the message. The person that tweeted it originally will be notified.

- **#FF** stands for **"Follow Friday."** Twitter users often suggest who others should follow on Fridays by tweeting with the hashtag #FF.

- **Mentioning another user** in your Tweet by including the @ sign followed directly by their username is called a "mention". Also refers to Tweets in which your username was included about replies and mentions.

- Reply is when a response to a posted tweet is sent, usually posted by clicking the "**reply**" button next to their Tweet in your timeline. Always begins with @username.

- **Top Tweets and Trending Topics** are determined by a Twitter algorithm to be the most popular or resonant on Twitter at any given time.

Twitter for Business

Be sure to set up a Twitter account and build out your profile. Make sure it is branded similarly to your website, LinkedIn Company profile and any other marketing and social media sites. Have your clients, vendors, friends and co-workers follow you, add a follow link to your website and your email signature and then get started!

1. **Identify keywords** that your prospects use both in their tweets and their profiles. There are a few ways to accomplish this. First, brainstorm words and pop them into search engines to see what comes up. Next, look at your clients' tweets and check out the keywords they are using, there is a good chance more people like them are using those words.

2. **Search those keywords** in Twitter in the search bar or through a social media scheduler such as HootSuite. Be sure to use quotation marks if your phrases are multiple words. Ex. "Human Resources" You will find many people similar to your client in a stream with real time results and recent updates.

3. Now it is time to **listen** to what they are saying. Evaluate if they are indeed someone you may be able to help, and if so follow them. You will learn what interests them, what kind of content they find valuable enough to share and you gain some insights on what matters to them.

4. **Send them some of your great content** with lead capture videos and downloads by mentioning them in a tweet. Ex. "Wanted to share this great HR blog on employee retention @SocialSalesLink URL".

5. Continue to deliver value by **retweeting their content** or identify their clients and recommend that others follow them in a combine mention - Great post by @kimgarst - Marketing Tips Specifically for #Authors http://bit.ly/HNGXV8" @Lyndonx.

6. **Follow your competitors' followers.** Don't go randomly but methodically, they are already people interested in your industry.

7. **Post thought provoking discussions** and ask for opinions in tweets with mentions. Create and share polls through tweets with mentions requests for votes and input from targeted prospects.

8. Once you have conversations and engagement, **take it offline** and begin to develop real relationships.

paywithatweet.com is one of the greatest tools when running a lead capture campaign. It is the best $2.99 per month imaginable. If you have a great download, rather than filling out a form, we are asking them to tweet our content out. Be sure to use #hashtags and links to your landing pages to get the most out of the share!

Facebook for Business

Facebook is primarily a consumer driven site, but is the largest online community. Even if people aren't conducting professional business here, they are hanging out, so let's make sure we have a solid presence. Here are the key components of having solid profiles:

1. Complete your company profile and brand it to match your website and marketing collateral.
2. Request that your friends follow your page.
3. Post all of your thought leadership, content and videos.
4. Share industry related content.
5. As your company page, "like" and comment on relevant information in your news stream.
6. Consider running contests to get more "likes".
7. As your company page, follow "like" and comment your prospects, strategic alliances and competitors followers.
8. If you are a B2B (business to business) company, weigh the time you spend on Facebook and ensure that you are getting an ROI on your time and resources. Typically, Facebook is great for commercial and consumer sales.

Google+ for Business

Google+ is so powerful, and so underutilized. It is one of the simplest platforms to truly find where the right people for you are hanging out. They have really made it easy to find communities of like-minded professionals where we can learn from, and share great content. It is simple to find where your target market is hanging out and begin to engage with them. Ultimately growing a strong network of professionals.

1. Log in to Google+.
2. From the home page, choose "communities" from the drop down.
3. In the search bar on the top right type in key words describing your target market.
4. Join the community.
5. Like and comment on the posts, or share them within Google+ or other platforms.
6. If you click "see all" on the right you can see profile pictures, click through and "ADD' to your circles.
7. Be sure to add them in a relevant circle, or add a new circle for your community subject.
8. In some of the larger communities you can choose a category on the right hand side of the "community".
9. If you choose Google+ profiles there are a lot of open invitations to connect (LinkedIn Profiles, Facebook, Pinterest and more).
10. Post in discussions and add #hashtags to get found.

Content Aggregators

Creating our own content is great, but often we are sharing other people's content as well. Sometimes it is a blog or article we come across, but wouldn't it be great if content were fed to us, especially targeted content that we care about? Well, use these tools and customize your newsfeed and make it easy to share.

1. Pulse
2. Feed.ly
3. Scoop.it
4. Google Alerts
5. Buzzfeed
6. Blogrunner
7. Digg
8. Stackla

Plus a CRM

Nimble is a cloud based CRM that automatically pulls your contacts into one place so you can engage them across any channel (LinkedIn, Twitter, Facebook, Google+, Skype, Phone, Email) in one interface. It eliminates most data entry, keeps your notes, reminders and follow ups syncing with your calendar, creates a listening platform that allows you to filter out the noise, has an integrated email and messaging platform and helps manage and report on the sales funnel.

Lead Capture Pages

Landing pages or squeeze pages are a fantastic way to capture leads. You can set them up yourself in a Wordpress site, or use professional pages that are engaging and have a high conversation rate. Some popular sites to create fabulous pages are:

1. Constant Contact or AWebber
2. Leadpages.net
3. Offerpop.com
4. Hubspot
5. Marketo
6. Ace of Sales (Jeffery Gittomer's Email system)

Social Sales Link's Blog Posts

Linkedinposts.com

Content Schedulers

If you have a social media strategy, it might make sense to get some help. There are programs that send out scheduled posts to any or all of your social media platforms. We tweet while we're sleeping! Most offer great reporting on engagement tools as well so you can track your activity. Here are three of the top aggregators:

1. HootSuite
2. SproutSocial
3. TweetDeck

URL Shorteners

These services help take longer URLs and transform them into manageable links that almost never exceed 20 characters. They can also track the number of clicks a link has, which offers great metrics for evaluating your social media strategies. A few popular shorteners are:

1. Bitly.com
2. Ow.ly
3. Tinyurl
4. Goo.gl

There are a lot of social media tools and without a doubt it is critical to decide what works best for you, your company and your business goals. Not everyone uses everything.

Cool Tools for the Advanced User

ClickToTweet.com – you create a tweet that you would like others to share, and clicktotweet creates a link that when clicked produces your tweet in their twitter update section, all they have to do is hit send. This is great for websites and email signatures.

LinkedIn share code makes it easy for your network to share your content on LinkedIn with one click. This is crazy powerful. You can generate a simple HTML code to share blogs, videos or any content from your website to anyone's LinkedIn profile or groups with one click. If you are not savvy at this, share the code with your web developer, they will customize it in minutes! WE LOVE THIS!

To get a copy and paste of this code please visit http://bit.ly/LIsharecode (case sensitive).

Your Plan

Schedule Management Tips

Managing your time comes from understanding your priorities and working through what needs to be done to meet your goal. Through the next few pages, we are going to be talking about goals a lot. The key for time management is to decide which of the activity goals will help you achieve the best results, and then focus on those.

1. Record your thoughts on your smart phone, tablet, notebook or pad of paper. Most of our great ideas can come to us at very inopportune times and then we forget them later. Be sure to catch them when you can and work on them later.

2. Create your action plan or to-do-list. Some people create a list every morning. Whether you create your list from scratch or roll it over from yesterday's list, it is important to determine what you need to do each day. Then think about what of those things are have to's and want to's. This will help you decide where to focus your energy.

3. Schedule your activity goals into your calendar and treat them like clients. If you had a client phone call, would you blow that off for something else that just popped up? Of course not. So, treat your activity goals like clients and you will get them done. The new goals you determine should go on your list and be given a priority.

4. Schedule time for the pop-ups. Every day, schedule a half an hour to 45-minute block in your calendar for your interruptions. If it happens to be a quiet day, you will have more time to get your want to's done.

5. Schedule a 15-minute buffer before and after every call. This gives you time for your pre-call planning. Visit your prospects LinkedIn profile, the company site, Google them, check out what they are tweeting about, and your prospects shared connections. Obviously when we get into full blown appointments, this could be an hour or longer process, but 15 minutes before every initial call can make a big difference in where the conversation leads. Be sure to write down your goal of the call and your desired next steps, so you can keep your eye on the prize. Schedule 15 minutes after the call to record your notes, ensure that your next steps are on the calendar and you have scheduled your follow-up work.

6. If you do not have a scheduled call and you are in the middle of an activity, don't answer the phone just because it rings. People expect calls to go to voicemail. Schedule two 30-minute blocks a day when you will return those calls.

7. Schedule two 30-minute blocks to answer email. This may seem like a lot, an hour a day just to respond to email, but if you actually add the up the time you are checking and answering now, it might save you an hour a day!

8. Lump your similar activities together. You can get so much more done with momentum. It is amazing how much more productive you can be by scheduling your time.

If you can adapt these 8 steps, you will see a huge impact in your productivity.

S.M.A.R.T. Goals

We believe that it is essential to have well-defined and strategic goals. In addition, we encourage our clients to write down their goals and to create them in the SMART format.

Let's look at this format and make sure your goals are in the proper format. SMART is an acronym for goals that are Specific, Measurable, Aligned, Realistic, and Timed. How many of us have said at some point in our life that we wanted to get in shape by the summer? But by the time the summer rolled around you were in the exact same shape? That is because it was not specific. If you said, that you wanted to lose 10 lbs. in a month, that might be a SMART Goal.
The end game here is to develop an activities goal plan – a check list of sorts that is drilled down to the most basic steps.

The best way to look at your plan is to imagine that you are going away for 3 months on an all expense paid vacation anywhere in the world. And in order for your business to thrive while you are gone, you are going to place someone in your spot with your same skill set. This person even has your same personality...

There are two types of goals: activity and results.

Activity Goals are what we are going to do. We have complete control over whether or not we accomplish these goals.

Results Goals are our best estimate of what our activities goals will achieve. We believe you must frame your activity goals around the results in order to accomplish them. For the sake of this exercise, you want to keep most of your goals Activity Goals, but keep the result in mind. In other words, we want to be sure that the activity is aligned with the results we want to achieve.

Now go back to your commitment list at the beginning of the book. Based on your vision, let's start organizing the "to do list". Put a priority around each of the items, decide if each is a SMART goal, and if not, make it one. Then determine if it is an Activity Goal or Results Goal. If it is an Activity Goal you want to add it to your Activity Goal sheet in the next couple of pages.

The next page is an example of the activities tracking form. Keeping this up to date and using it consistently will be a key piece to your success. You can certainly create a spreadsheet to track the activity. It works exceptionally well.

Specific

Measurable

Aligned

Realistic

Timed

LinkedIn Only Example Goals

Activity	Daily	Weekly	M	T	W	Th	F	A/R
Request to connect with current clients	1	5	-	-	3	-	2	A
Connect with current prospects	1	5	1	2	-	1	1	A
Connect with past clients & prospects	1	5	5	-	-	-	-	A
Connect with SA* on LinkedIn	1	5	2	1	1	1	-	A
Meet with SRS and exchange intros		1	-	-	-	-	1	R
Request intros from saved searches	2	10	-	10	-	-	-	A
Identify client connections		2	2	-	-	-	-	A
Ask for client introductions		1	-	-	1	-	-	A
Prospect meetings		3	1	-	1	-	1	R
Make introductions for others	1	5	1	1	1	1	1	A
Post to home page		1	1	-	-	-	-	A
Engage others in groups (like/comment)	2	10	1	5	2	1	1	A
Post to groups		1	1	-	-	-	-	A
Content in the inbox of group members	10	50	-	50	-	-	-	A
Research companies before calling	2	10	2	2	2	2	2	A
Blog		1	1	-	-	-	-	A
Create polls in groups		1	-	-	-	1	-	A
Join a new group		1	-	1	-	-	-	A
Read LinkedIn Today	1	5	1	1	1	1	1	A
Check out LinkedIn Signal		1	-	-	1	-	-	A
Proposals from LinkedIn activity		1	-	-	-	-	1	R
New clients (this could be monthly or quarterly depending on your sales cycle)		1	1	-	-	-	-	R

*SA = Strategic Alliance or Center of Influence. A person who you can network to make introductions on each others' behalf. Be sure they work within the same industry, share the same decision maker as you, but is not a competitor.

LinkedIn & Social Selling For Business Development

Your Goals

Activity	Daily	Weekly	M	T	W	Th	F	A/R

Social Selling Strategy

Are you looking to fill your sales funnel with qualified leads on a consistent basis? Well, if you made it this far in the book, we are going to assume that your answer is a YES!

But knowing what to do, what to say and when to do it often seems to get in the way of actually getting it done. Knowing all of this information is just not enough. Now it is time to put it into practice.

Okay, we have to let you down easy; there is not one right strategy that we can teach because every company and need is different. But, what you will get is all the elements and our strategy and plan as an example. If you are feeling a little overwhelmed at developing your plan, this is an opportunity to work with a professional goal setter or sales trainer to ensure that what you commit to is realistic and on target. You may find however, that you have it covered! Either way, the next steps are about taking all you have learned, developing a strategy and plan, and then putting it to work to attract and engage targeted qualified prospects on a consistent basis.

First, what is a strategy? Dictionary please…

noun • a plan of action or policy designed to achieve a major or overall aim.

Many think strategy is just the big picture and that tactics are the plan of action, but according to Webster, a strategy is a plan to achieve a goal, not just defining the goal. Why do we point this out? If we focus just on big picture achievement, we rarely get there without breaking down the results and activity goals. So we will cover both of them!

Begin with the End in Mind

What is it you would like to achieve? This is definitely the big picture piece. Here's the big question, if we were to talk a year from now and you said – this was an amazing social media year for our company – what happened that made it so good for you? When you can answer this question, you can build out your plan. Review all your options that you have learned in this book and others. Look at what others are doing in your industry and related ones and try some of what you see. If you have a good plan in place, you will be able to measure what is working and what isn't.

Goals and Objectives

What do you want to achieve big picture question:
- Brand awareness/PR
- SEO/Website Traffic
- Customer interaction/Visitor Loyalty
- Lead Generation/Conversion rate
- Conversations/engagement
- E-commerce
- Education
- Market Research
- Advocacy
- Entertainment
- Grow a mailing list

Build out a realistic view of where you would like to see the Social Selling results in 3, 6, 9, 12 months.

Listen

You can't begin a solid strategy without knowing your client and what they need and want. Determine where your customers are hanging out, LinkedIn Groups, Fan pages, twitter, Google+ groups and go hang out with them. What are they talking about? What are they sharing on twitter and in posts? Read what they care about and talk to the points that will engage them. Don't just limit your search to your client or prospects, look at the market conditions and their competition too.

If you look at a company page on LinkedIn, "People also viewed" and you will get a list of companies similar to the one you are visiting. There are some great insights here and the big bonus is adding new-targeted prospects to your list.

Look at #tagboard to follow keywords and phrases and gives you a dashboard of real-time share across the major social media platforms. Don't forget to research your clients' competition, market conditions and industry.

While doing all of this research, create content topics that these people find both valuable and engaging, and would therefore want to share with others. Read the full articles and blogs and just write down the topics. This will give you a solid place to start creating content later.

Define Your Goal

Stephen R. Covey said, "Begin with the end in mind" and that is brilliant. Your social media plan works much better when you are not throwing tweets on the wall hoping some will stick.

Social Selling Tools

There are so many social media options out that it may be hard to decide which is right for you. As far as picking social platforms for businesses, start with the big ones for sure – LinkedIn, Twitter, Facebook, Google+ and maybe YouTube if you have video. If you have a visual product or service, add in Pinterest and Instagram for sure. The others will pop up occasionally; you can evaluate them and see if your prospects are hanging out there. As for tools, that is a whole other story. Tools can make or break your campaign. At minimum, have a blog to share your content and use a scheduler like HootSuite.

Create Your Platforms

Define your look, the feel you want to evoke and keep within your overall branding efforts. Your platforms should have their own personalities and should feel unified and cohesive. Not the artist for the job? Then the task is a very simple one to outsource.

Commit Time & Resources

Unfortunately there is no pixie dust. There has to be a clear activity plan with specified time and delegation. Who is going to do what? – And when? You can refer to the schedule on the next few pages when developing your company's strategy and execution plan. There are many different responsibilities when it comes to a successful social media plan. The following is a general list. Check the ones that are relevant to you and your business and assign ownership of them.

- Develop and update social media policies and best practices including branding guide lines.
- Determine the social platforms you will use
- Create Content
- Video / Photos
- Approve Content
- Who uploads the content
- Research, choose and test social tools
- Coordinate the schedule
- Assign accountability partners to keep each other on task
- Designate an implementer
- Have a solid process in place
- Follow the right people on the right channels #tagboard is a great source
- Assign an answerer of questions
- Determine who will do the targeted engagement
- Who will follow up on web leads or what is the process
- Offer support and help either internally or from an outside company that can guide the process initially

Delegate, Outsource and Assign Ownership

Although it is difficult to give up all social media responsibilities, there are many you can have others run on your behalf. If you have an assistant or intern, consider assigning some of the social selling activities to them. Many of the activities can be shared as well.

Be sure to assign ownership to every task. If it is clear who owns each project and who is ultimately responsible for the activities getting done, there is a greater chance of success.

If you can develop a step-by-step process for each activity, it makes the program very easy to follow, scale, as well as train others.

Activity	Owner/ Responsibility	Steps
Client and/or Strategic Alliance Introduction Requests	Shared	1. Assistant identifies who the client knows that meets criteria 2. You drill down, choose 4-5 and ask the client
Creating Content	Shared	1. Record ideas – either on paper, email or voice recorder 2. Develop a blog template 3. Assistant can take ideas and fill in the template and adds a call to action 4. You edit 5. Assistant posts and schedules
Sharing Content	Assistant or shared	1. Schedule Your Content 2. Aggregate content and schedule and share 3. Share whenever something inspires you 4. Follow, like and share content of your prospects, clients and networking partners

Outsourcing can be great, but choose your partner carefully. There are tons of companies popping up everywhere that are implementing social media for their clients, but not all have social selling in mind. Be sure that the work is relevant to your buyer, it is purposeful, and that success can be measured by creating engagement with qualified prospects, generating leads and driving more sales.

Determine Your Schedule

Use a shared Google calendar, Google Docs or Dropbox to keep track of the schedule and make it accessible to all the parties that are involved. This is a good way to keep everyone accountable for his or her respective commitments.

Our prospecting plan from scratch:

We are going to keep this very clear and concise and in order of development. Before we start we have to get the foundation in place. This outline may be the most powerful tool in the entire book!

- Find your SEO Keyword that will be used throughout all your pages
- Research what your competitors are doing right and wrong. Also, even if they aren't in your industry, identify styles of writing and branding that fit your personality
- Find bloggers in your space, later on we might want to try guest blogging
- Create a blog (mine is in my website) that includes:
- Social Sharing buttons from AddThis
- Comments that need moderation
- No dates – much of our content is recyclable. We just change the calls to action. If someone receives a blog with a date from a year ago, they will most likely ignore it or even worse, notice that you sent the old information.
- SEO plug in so that we can add the key words and descriptions to help the web browsers find our content easier
- Forms for download – I use formidable forms and love it. When someone downloads content, it can email it to them, redirect them and I immediately get an email with my new lead
- Register and build out, brand and customize the URL for the social platforms that make sense for your business I chose:
- LinkedIn Personal Profile
- LinkedIn Company Profile
- Twitter
- Facebook pages
- Google+
- Google Maps (if you have a physical location)
- YouTube
- External Tools
- Wistia for our video – Wistia offers heat mapping and opt-in that creates immediate leads. It even integrates with auto-responders.
- A URL shortener and tracker program, we use Bit.Ly
- HootSuite for scheduling
- Dropbox and Google Docs for collaboration
- Box.net and Slideshare for uploading documents that we want to share with others through a link. This is very good to use if you don't have a blog but want to share content. Your viewers can actually download your content.

- Constant Contact for emailing – they also have some great social campaigns for Facebook and Twitter, but we tend to use offerpop.com for that.
- TextExpander is our favorite! This makes our world so much easier. It may be the best $35 we have ever spent. Type more with less effort! TextExpander saves from typing the same thing over and over again. It is simply setting up custom keyboard shortcuts into frequently used text and pictures so when the shortcut is typed the entire message appears. We use this in tons of ways but most frequently to acknowledge our new followers and for our introduction requests.
- Sign up for Google Authorship, it is a complicated process, but if you become a blogger and thought leader, this will help your followers find all your content in one place.
- Create educational and engaging white papers for downloading. Upload as a media file to your website and use the URL.
- Create opt-in landing pages on the site that collect name, email, phone, twitter handle etc. in exchange for your white paper.
- Videos – have a welcome video and an educational video at the minimum, not only does it engage your visitors, but it helps your SEO
- Write your white paper and 5 blogs for launch
- Post
- Schedule in HootSuite
- Share your content on your social media pages
- Target posts (spearfish marketing)
- Share on twitter with directly mentioning your prospects (twitter strategy to follow in the next few pages)
- Share with targeted prospects in groups, as we discussed earlier
- Post your content to non-competitor Facebook pages where your prospects are fans
- Partner with your networking friends to "like" and share each others' content so Google see you as relevant
- Follow thought leaders and share their stuff with your commentary
- Use Pulse or Scoop.it to make that so much easier
- Comment with links to your blog (only when relevant)
- Ask the thought leaders to guest blog for you and maybe they will reciprocate
- Follow-up on leads
- If we received their twitter handle, we follow and try to favorite or ReTweet a post of theirs (please read what you are sharing first!)
- We find them on LinkedIn, send out a connections request with a personal message thanking them for downloading our stuff and that we would like to schedule a time to talk (if they are indeed a prospect). Once we connect, we take notes on their profile and tag them in their respective categories.
- Set a reminder.

The following is the schedule to manage the weekly activity goals.

Social Selling Example Plan

My social selling goal is to get information about my prospects needs and initiatives even before we meet. This is best served with larger more complex deals if your product or service is a low dollar amount, modify the time invested proportionately to the pre-call planning state.

Pre-Call Planning for Insights Selling

On LinkedIn connect with the people that will be at the meeting and go through the Rapport Building Exercise. Be sure to reach out to shared connections!

Make a list of the titles of all potential influencers and decision makers within the organization. If you have had a similar client before, look at all the titles you touched during the sales process.

Look up LinkedIn Company Page and identify what they have posted, and try to find all the names that match the titles, check out their profiles but hold off on connecting with them. If you have any connections already, drop them a note and let them know I will be there for a meeting and that if they are available I would like to pop my head in and say hello.

- Check out Products and Services Tab
- If they have a featured LinkedIn Group listed, go join it
- Look at people who have viewed this company also viewed – they are often competition

Check out their news on Google, press releases, website posts and blog.

Research the industry conditions, news, articles and the market.

Identify people in my network that are in the industry, reach out and have a conversation.

Look at prospects new connections, you may be able to identify who you will be up against, if I am connecting with a prospect prior to an initial meeting, so is my competition.

Join my client's industry specific group and ask questions to learn more about the conditions and innovations happening in their world.

LinkedIn & Social Selling For Business Development

My prospecting goal, to get qualified leads from people who download or opt-in to my content. Here is my strategy.

Activity	Frequency
CONTENT: Blog/Vlog	2x Week
Whitepaper for download w/ landing page for web leads	1x Month
HOOTSUITE SCHEDULE: • Twitter post content and videos from your library 5x per day with different hash tags and mentions of your prospects and clients • Through custom streams with thought leaders and prospects, identify 20 posts and schedule to share randomly – put in your own commentary and share on Twitter and Facebook page • Follow back your new followers and thank them for the follow • From # stream follow 10 new people • Acknowledge mentions and RT • Share newest blogs on all platforms including LinkedIn Groups	1x Week
Facebook As your company, "Like" 5 new thought leader or prospects pages engage in 5 conversations on other pages with likes and comments – share your blog when appropriate	1x Week
Scoop.it, Pulse, Feed.ly, Google and Tagboard Find and share 2 blogs and add your own commentary	2x Day
LinkedIn • Spearfish in groups – 25 targeted message to direct emails with each new • For networking partners and clients this week identify the names of people you want to meet and ask for introductions • Ask for intros from saved searches • Look up 1 new prospective company, find someone in common and ask for introductions • Participate in one discussion from a group or update in your newsfeed • Schedule next steps with new connections • Post to 50 groups – 10 per day • Post a poll to groups – 1x Monthly	1x Day
Prospect, Networking Partner and/or Client • Follow all of their social media platforms • Connect on LinkedIn • "like", comment, share or RT a post • Share your blog in a mention	With each new relationship
Email Campaign: • Pick your best blog and a call to action • Free webinars and announcements no more than 1x Month • Advertising should be at a minimum, you need to provide value first	1x Week
Reach out to guest bloggers • Invite thought leaders to guest blog • Request a guest blogger on popular sites	10 per month
Google+ • Join a communities • Add prospects and networking people to circles and follow companies • "Like" and comment on other blogs • Post blogs and videos on profile and communities	1x Day

Keep this in a spreadsheet or CRM reoccurring task list. And have someone keep you accountable for the goals.

Extra Credit

Log Out of LinkedIn NOW

I learned something new about LinkedIn today - you can see where you are logged in. I thought I would see 3 computers that I was currently logged into; my phone, laptop and iPad, but boy was I shocked when I saw I was still logged in 48 places over the last 4 months. How crazy is that?! I am walking with my head down in shame! Did I really forget to log out of all of those computers?

I teach every day in public venues and private companies, and I seem to not be logging out. Well, thanks to the #linkedinchat I participated in tonight, I have now learned how to remotely log out of all those accounts, and I would like to share those steps with you tonight:

From the Your active sessions page, you can see how many sessions you're currently signed into. https://www.linkedin.com/settings/sessions

On that page, you can also review all devices that are signed in to your LinkedIn account, when you last signed in, what browser was used, the IP address, and the city and state the login occurred.

To view your sessions:

1. Hover over your profile photo on the top right of your homepage and select Privacy & Settings.
   - You may be prompted to sign in.

2. Click See where you've logged in at the top section under Your active sessions.

To sign out of a session:

1. Click Sign out to the right of the session you'd like to end.
2. Click Sign out to confirm.

To sign out of every active session (except your current one):

1. Click Sign out of all these sessions at the top of your list.
2. Click Sign out to confirm.

If you are logged into sessions in places you don't recognize, consider changing your password!

Who Owns the Content You Post on LinkedIn?

Often when we publish content to a third party site, we give up ownership. In fact, until Facebook updated their Statement of Rights and Responsibilities in November 2013 it was very unclear on their rights to our pictures, videos and intellectual property that we shared on their site. Now, it is stated that we own the rights but they can use it. In addition they now allow privacy settings that give us control over who in our network can see our content.

Twitter's Terms of Services allows us retain our rights as well as any content we submit, post or display. However, we do agree to grant them a worldwide, non-exclusive, royalty-free license to use, copy, reproduce, process, adapt, modify, publish, transmit, display and distribute such content in any and all media or distribution methods. So although we still own it, they can practically do anything they want with it.

In LinkedIn's User Agreement, it is currently not clear if our photos, updates, posts, presentations, comments or any other content we share is ours or theirs. It doesn't specifically agree to not use our content for their own purposes. It even doesn't agree to stop sharing content that you have deleted. So should you be nervous?

Nope...LinkedIn is updating their User Agreement effective October 23, 2014 to reinforce their commitment to respecting what's ours. They are officially giving us control and ownership of our content.

Just remember, no matter what, once you put something out on the internet, it is public. Even deleting posts doesn't mean it will permanently go away. So, only share information you are fine with the whole world seeing...just in case they do!

TIP: If you are blogging your intellectual capital, you may want to add a copyright on the bottom of all of your posts, it may protect you against other's poaching your content.

DISCLOSURE: I am not an attorney, so if copyright and trade marking is important to you, let me know and I will introduce you to an attorney that can help.

6 Amazing Ways to Use the LinkedIn Apps

1. On the classic Linkedin App you can now customize an invitation to connect! When you are on the profile page, there is a box with an arrow on the very top of the screen. This allows you to follow them, customize an invitation or forward their profile. This is such a big deal and I am beyond thrilled that personal invites can now happen via the App. By the way, you don't need an email or to choose "how you know them" when connecting here.

2. From the classic Linkedin App you can download your LinkedIn connections to your address book. A new contact will be created after LinkedIn tries to match the contacts so not to create a duplicate. If they find a match it will complete open fields but not replace existing ones, so you won't lose your current data. And, each time you launch the app, LinkedIn will ask you if you would like to update your address book with your new connections. What a great way to keep your contacts current!

3. The LinkedIn Connected App makes it very easy to sync your calendar and then it alerts you when you are meeting or have met someone you aren't connected to yet. It makes getting ready and following up on a meeting uber easy!

4. From the LinkedIn Connected app you can wish happy birthdays and congratulations to your connections fast and simple. To make semi-customized messages easier, use keyboard shortcuts. On the iPhone go to Settings, Keyboard, Shortcuts and add clever phrases that you can share with a few keystrokes so your message will stand out for the 187 other ones they have received and it will keep your connections appreciating you.

5. The LinkedIn Pulse App delivers news based on my settings. It has actually saved me money, really. How? Usually when I am standing in the grocery store line I get sucked in to the gossipy magazines, but now I go right to the Pulse App and read content that I really enjoy!

6. If you are using LinkedIn Navigator (premium account), you can quickly see the leads that you have previously saved, view what they are talking about in one newsfeed and engage with them in real-time, even if you aren't connected to them yet.

If you aren't using the LinkedIn Apps because you never tried them or because you tried them and found them sketchy at best, try them again...you might be quite surprised!

Creating a Prospecting List by Company

As sales coaches we make sure that our clients have their top 50 list of companies that they are pursuing at all times. With LinkedIn you can create that list with already having an edge…a warm connection. Through LinkedIn's filters, building your top prospecting list couldn't be easier.

Here is how:

1. Hover over Interest and click on Companies
2. Click on the center tab Search Companies
3. Drill away

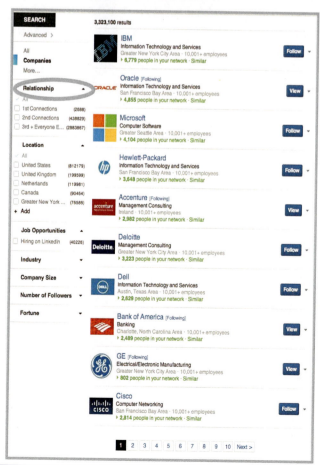

LinkedIn & Veterans

LinkedIn is offering assistance and education to help veterans find new career paths and job positions through the power of its network and immense search engine. The commitment they have shown is not only patriotic, but it is making a huge impact for veterans, who have served their country, to get back into the workforce.

Veterans are a valuable asset to any business. Companies around the country are recognizing this and creating special programs designed specifically for hiring Veterans. Veterans are naturally imbued with leadership, critical thinking skills, and are among the most dedicated workers. By electing to serve their country, they're demonstrating and indeed living by a set of values any employer would find attractive. The Army uses the acronym LDRSHIP to define its core values. Aside from the obvious undertones of leadership, the acronym stands for the following: Loyalty - Veterans demonstrate a commitment to their fellow team members and organizations that is unparalleled in the civilian sector. Duty - Veterans always place the mission (whether it be as involved as complex combat operations, or as simple as sending out a weekly memo, above themselves. Respect - Respect doesn't just mean to respect figures of authority, but to treat fellow soldiers, co-workers, fellow man, with dignity and respect. Selfless Service - Closely linked to duty, selfless service, simply put, means that Veterans will always go above and beyond what is asked and expected of them. Honor - Honor is about more than just gallantry and accolades won in the heat of battle. Honor means living these values day in day out, regardless of where life takes you. Integrity - The code of ethics ingrained in every soldier, sailor, and airmen, means that by hiring a Veteran, you're hiring someone you will always be able to trust to do what's right, both legally and morally. Finally, Personal Courage - Courage isn't something that's limited to the battlefield. It takes guts to give a superior the hard facts he needs, but might not want, so that he can make the right decisions. Veterans have been taught to face those fears and overcome them, making them the ideal candidate for high leverage, high stress business environments.

Loyalty, Duty, Respect, Selfless Service, Honor, Integrity, and Personal Courage. Do these characteristics sound like someone you might want to work at your company? While the LDRSHIP acronym was designed by the Army, all the service branches have similar values and they're indicative of the quality of individual that decides to put on the uniform. While not necessarily gaining any direct applicable skills during their service, these soft skills are invaluable to building a great company. Linkedin recognizes the potential veterans have and developed a number of services designed to help Veterans craft their profiles and connect them to future employers. The Veteran Mentor Network Group on LinkedIn is an initiative designed to connect veterans to other veterans in positions of leadership to help them get to where they want to be professionally. There are many ways to connect to Veterans in your community. Utilizing LinkedIn's resources, as well as reaching out to the Student Veterans of America, the nation's leading Student Veterans Organization, and getting in touch with Veteran leaders from your local institutions of higher learning, is a great place to start getting connected.

Walter Tillman (linkedin.com/in/waltertillman) is former President of the Student Veterans Association at Arizona State University and founding member of the Arizona Student Veterans Coalition. He has been invited to speak at national conferences on creating sustainable student veterans organizations, and how to maximize the reach of those organizations. For information on his specific organization you can go to www.ASUTempeVets, or follow their progress through their organization's social media sources at www.facebook.com/ASUTempeVets or www.twitter.com/ASUTempeVets.com

Alumni

Every school's Alumni page includes powerful search options and filters that can quickly help you find other professionals that went to your school. This aligns perfectly with the Social Sales Link philosophies of warm market connections. You can easily find people you went to school with or even identify where alumni are now that may be able to help you get into companies are your prospecting list. The filters are as follows:

1. The years they were in school.
2. Where they live now.
3. Where they work.
4. Their positions at work.
5. What they studied in school.
6. Their listed skills.
7. How are you connected (1st, 2nd, 3rd or Group)

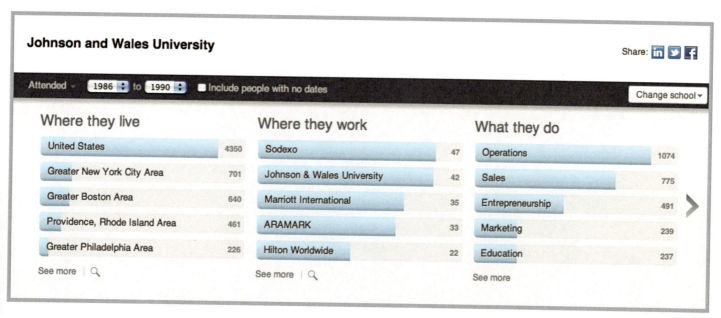

Menu Options

LinkedIn has a lot of hidden gems. Explore the bar at the bottom of your LinkedIn profile, it has a wonderful help center (www.help.linkedin.com), blog link and additional tools that are worth checking out.

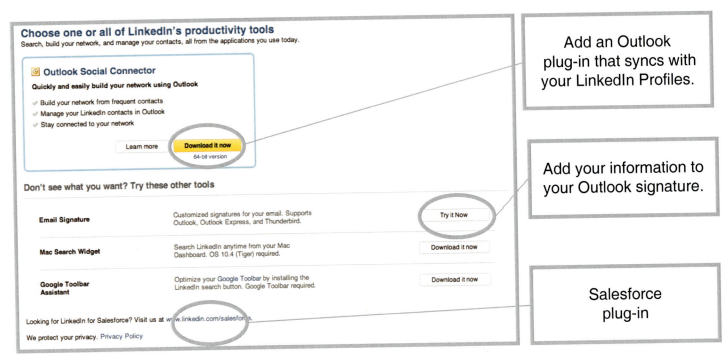

Add an Outlook plug-in that syncs with your LinkedIn Profiles.

Add your information to your Outlook signature.

Salesforce plug-in

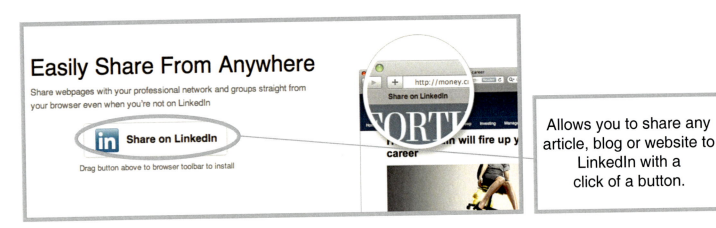

Allows you to share any article, blog or website to LinkedIn with a click of a button.

Job Seeker

LinkedIn is best known for its job seeking opportunities. Much of what we learned throughout this workbook can be translated into job searching mode. Finding a job is, for all intents and purposes the ultimate sales position. You are selling yourself.

However, LinkedIn has a few fantastic job seeking advanced search functions that make it very simple to see postings that companies use when they are in hiring mode.

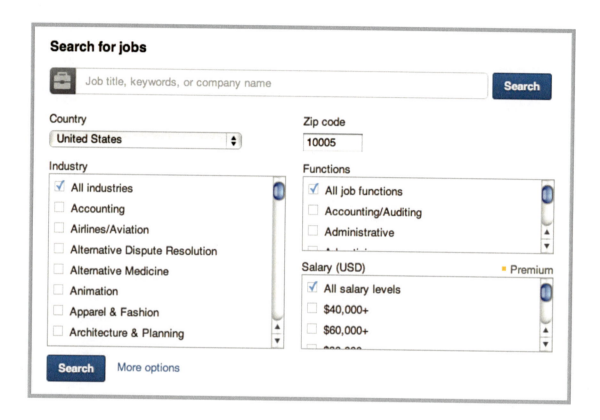

If you are a consultant or a company that offers outsourced services such as IT, CFO, Accounting this is prime for identifying openings. You can quickly convert the conversation from the need for the company to hire a full time person to hiring you.

LinkedIn for CEOs

CEOs using LinkedIn are getting more effective hires, more sales, and better use of their networks because LinkedIn helps them manage relationships.

We have 5 Tips to help CEOs grow company sales through LinkedIn:

1. Leverage your staff's network. - You, the management team and non-selling staff should connect to the sales team on LinkedIn so that they can benefit from the entire staff's network. If your salespeople are calling on a new prospect, (s)he searches for the company on LinkedIn, identifies that you or one of your employee's LinkedIn connections knows the decision maker there. (S)he can ask for a warm introduction and ultimately leverage the power of the company's network to build his/her relationship with the prospect. This helps your salesperson get in front of the decision maker faster, reduces the sales cycle and increases the close ratio.

2. Hire better sales people. The best sales people are rarely unemployed or even in the job market, so they aren't answering job ads or have their resumes listed on job boards. As a result, many of your best sales hires come from employee, client, or network referrals. With LinkedIn you can leverage your network to find the best, most suited hires for your company.

3. Collect competitive intelligence. Contacting former employees of specific companies is a great way to conduct competitive research. By creating advanced searches for a company and selecting "past" from the dropdown menu, you will get a list of people who formerly worked at that company. If you are looking for talent from specific companies, this may be a great way of recruiting employees with the experience you are looking for.

4. Leverage Board of Directors. Often, CEOs are challenged with getting their Board Members to bring in new business opportunities regardless of the fact that they are assigned that responsibility. Prior to each meeting with a Director, have you or your assistant look them up on LinkedIn and identify 2-3 connections that are good leads for your organization and ask for introductions to you or your sales team.

5. Position yourself as a "Thought Leader". The first step is to be sure you have a complete profile with video and content. Next, be sure to have consistent updates with pertinent industry information that can be posted by you, an assistant or even your marketing department. This activity positions you as a subject matter expert and in turn, brands your company in your industry.

It is critical that the leadership team of an organization takes control of their online presences and leverages it for the competitive advantage.

Compare Accounts

Almost everything in this workbook is based on the free LinkedIn account. However, there are some great features and benefits of some of the paid functionality. Below is a chart of what you get with upgrades. We tell our clients that if you are hitting walls, clicking on links and seeing messages from LinkedIn saying "If you want to see that, upgrade" it might be time. Just make sure you will use it.

Feature	Free	Business $24.95 / month	Sales Navigator $39.95 / month	Sales Executive $74.95 / month
InMail- Contanct anyone directly	X	3 per month	10 per month	25 per month
# of profiles seen in a single search	100	300	500	700
See full profile for entire network	X	Yes	Yes	Yes
Full list of who has viewed your profile	X	Yes	Yes	Yes
Lead Builder	X	X	Yes	Yes
Save notes on profiles	X	5 folders	25 folders	50 folders
Saved searches and alerts	3	5 weekly	7 weekly	10 weekly
Get introduced feature	5	15 outstanding	25 outstanding	35 outstanding
Allow all to send you an OpenLink Message	X	Yes	Yes	Yes

Is Premium Worth It?

We could never go back to the free account - but it is up to you decide. Here are the 6 reasons we love being a LinkedIn Premium member:

1. More saved searches.
2. Full names of all LinkedIn members not just our 1st and 2nds.
3. 90 day access of who has viewed our profile.
4. OpenLink - allows free InMail messages to any OpenLink Network member, even if they are outside of your network. Anyone on LinkedIn can send an OpenLink message to these Premium members without an Introduction or paying for an InMail.
5. We are able to see up to 300 results in my searches (basic is only 100).
6. The advanced search filters are AMAZING!

Advanced Social Media Users

URL Shorteners

URL shortening is a technique on the Internet in which a Uniform Resource Locator (URL) can be shorted in length and still direct to the required page. This is achieved by using a redirecting a domain address. For example, the URL "http://en.wikipedia.org/wiki/URL_shortening" can be shortened to "http://bit.ly/urlwiki", "http://tinyurl.com/urlwiki", "http://is.gd/urlwiki" or "http://goo.gl/Gmzqv".

This is especially convenient for messaging technologies such as Twitter and LinkedIn, which limits the number of characters that may be used in a message. Short URLs allow otherwise long web addresses to be referred to in a tweet. Another great benefit is that sites like bit.ly help you track how many click throughs you are getting for any given link.

Box.net along with SlideShare and Drop Box are great ways to upload documents, spreadsheets .pdf files and so much more. It will create a link that makes sharing these files as easy a click. You can add these to your LinkedIn profile, share the link in groups and use it anywhere that you would like others to access your files and an attachment option is not available. Box.net has a special feature in that it notifies you when someone has downloaded your document. If this was a link in your profile, you can quickly go to "WHO'S VIEWED YOUR PROFILE?" and there is a good chance you can identify the person who did.

Social Sharing

If you like how you can share prewritten tweets visit: http://clicktotweet.com/

If you want to create a link that allows others to share your content on LinkedIn- it takes a little coding but is a great tool! Visit: http://bit.ly/LIShareCode (case sensitive)

LinkedIn Bookmarklet

You can use the Sharing Bookmarklet to conveniently share articles and websites with your LinkedIn network directly from your browser.

1. Click **Tools** at the bottom of your profile page.
2. Click the **Sharing Bookmarklet** tab at the top of the page.
3. Drag and drop the **Share on LinkedIn** button to your browser toolbar to install.

Best Practices

LinkedIn Professional Community Guidelines – Straight from LinkedIn's Best Practices Page
What types of discussions and content are acceptable on LinkedIn?

LinkedIn is a company that aims to put its members first when it comes to making important decisions. Millions of professional conversations and shared insights are being exchanged every day on LinkedIn. To ensure these discussions help our members be more productive and successful, LinkedIn has put in place Professional Community Guidelines outlining the types of discussions and content that are acceptable on LinkedIn, and what may be deemed inappropriate and stopped by LinkedIn. These community guidelines are intended to provide our members guidance and complement the list of Do's and Don'ts found in the User Agreement governing your use of, and participation in, LinkedIn's online services.

Be Real. Unlike some other online services, our members need to be real people, who provide their real names and accurate information about themselves. It is not okay to provide misleading information about yourself, your qualifications or your work experience, affiliations or achievements on LinkedIn's service.

Be Professional. We ask our members to behave professionally by not being dishonest or inappropriate. We acknowledge the value of discussions around professional activities, but we do not want you to use LinkedIn to shock or intimidate others. It is not okay to share graphic images to shock others, and it is not okay to share obscene images or pornography on LinkedIn's service.

Be Nice. LinkedIn shouldn't be used to harm others. It is not okay to use LinkedIn's services to harass, abuse, or send other unwelcomed communications to people (e.g., junk mail, spam, chain letters, phishing schemes). Do not use LinkedIn's services to threaten violence or property damage, or for hate speech acts like attacking people because of their race, ethnicity, national origin, gender, sexual orientation, political or religious affiliations, or medical or physical condition. Also, please don't use LinkedIn's services to intentionally infect others with viruses, worms, or other software that can destroy or interrupt their data or computer devices. It is not okay to interfere or disrupt LinkedIn's service.

Respect Other's Rights and Follow the Law. We do not want LinkedIn to be used for illegal activities or to violate the rights of others. Don't use LinkedIn's services to commit fraud. Before sharing or using someone else's copyrighted works, trademarks, private information, or trade secrets, please make sure you have the legal right to do so.

Respect LinkedIn's Rights. Please don't violate the rights of LinkedIn. You can find more information about what this means in our User Agreement, but put simply, please don't use LinkedIn's services to wrongfully take data or information. It is not okay to suggest that you are affiliated with or endorsed by LinkedIn when you are not, and it is not okay to violate LinkedIn's intellectual property rights.

Congratulations

So that was a lot of information to grasp, but you have to admit, this is far better than cold calling. And, the tools to position you as a thought leader and the expert in your field will make a huge impact on growing your business.

Remember, you have access to watch the on-demand webinar over and over again. Take advantage of that, it will help you navigate LinkedIn and implement many of these strategies.

Keep an eye out for our new blogs and updates as well - check back every couple of weeks for the new features and SSL strategies that continually roll out.

Now, take a deep breath and start with your plan.

You have the secret now. LinkedIn and social selling is an incredibly effective way to grow your sales funnel, position yourself as the industry leader, reduce your sales cycle and close more business. The only mistake you can make is not implementing the new skill set you now possess. Just by working your way through this book, you are now more knowledgeable about LinkedIn and social selling than 99% of its members. You now have all the tools and strategies that have helped countless Social Sales Link professionals succeed - and you can too.

We would love to hear your success stories so that we can share them with our clients at our speaking engagements, in our marketing materials and on our website. We would also appreciate it if you could fill out the evaluation form and get it back to us. You could win a free SSL LIVE webinar for yourself and 23 of your closest friends and co-workers – now that is pretty cool!

If you are looking for direction, or help with developing your strategy and plan, or even help implementing your plan, we can help, that is what we do. Be sure to give us a call 800.401.8412 or email me directly at brynne.tillman@socialsaleslink.com and we can explore ways that we can work together. If you would like to build on this great information you can bring us into your company for a live LinkedIn Class, virtual webinar series or ask us about our monthly subscription service.

We wish you good networking!

LinkedInWebinar.info

Webinar Password: SSL

LinkedIn & Social Selling For Business Development

Evaluation

Social Sales Link
Better Leads | More Business

Your Feedback is Important to Us

Please hand in today, fax to 888.775.5262 or email
brynne.tillman@socialsaleslink.com

Name	Company	Date
Phone	Email Address	
Title	# of Sales People in Your Company	

Did this program meet your expectations? Not at All 1 2 3 4 5 6 7 8 9 10 Completely
Will you use LinkedIn to grow your business? Not at All 1 2 3 4 5 6 7 8 9 10 Completely

We are always looking to improve, what might you recommend?

[   ]

These are some sales challenges I am currently facing.

[   ]

☐ I am interested in speaking with someone from SSL about my social selling strategy

☐ My company could benefit from a private class or webinar

☐ I would be willing to write a recommendation for SSL

- By filling out this form you are agreeing to have an SSL representative contact you and be added to SSL's mailing list.

Linkedin.com/in/brynnetillman | SocialSalesLink.com | 888.775.5262
Copyright © 2013 Social Sales Link, LLC – All rights reserved.

Made in the USA
San Bernardino, CA
22 February 2015